discover the life

#6 in the life-giving lifestyle series:
a reader for small groups
applying the 4 life-giving practices

Copyright © 2007
All Rights Reserved

All rights reserved. No part of this book may be reproduced in any form, except for the inclusion of brief quotations in a review, without permission in writing from the author or publisher.

Scripture taken from the NEW AMERICAN STANDARD BIBLE®, Copyright © 1960, 1962m 1963, 1968, 1971, 1973, 1975, 1977, 1995 by the Lockman Foundation.
Used by permission.

First printing September, 2007
2nd Edition printing, October, 2010

Please visit our website at:
www.simplelivinginc.net

Published by Simple Living, Incorporated

Printed in the United States by Catalyst Graphics
1060 Lone Oak Road, Suite 140
Egan, MN 55121
651-452-2403

-dtl-
contents

what am i getting myself into?	page 5
week #1	page 9
week #2	page 23
week #3	page 34
week #4	page 42
week #5	page 54
week #6	page 61
appendix #1: A Life-giver's Covenant	page 71
appendix #2: How do I do Life-giving Truth without **dtl**?	page 73
appendix #3: 50 tips for effective groups	page 75
appendix #4: Discovering Life-giving Truth... ...on your own ...as a way of life.	page 80

for the bored
...the thoughtful
...the complex
...the religious
...the rebel
...the mature
...the brand new
...the yet-to-believe
...the pastor
...the teacher
...the elder
...the agnostic
...the empty
...the seasoned
...the cynical
...the disciple-maker
...the influencer
...the dutiful
...the hungry
...the visionary
...the full-hearted
...the hopeful

Seriously, dtl is for anybody and everybody who is hungry for growth at a heart level. None of these ideas are new, really, but the applications truly are. It's not a one time study that you complete, it's a lifestyle you adopt.

what am i getting myself into?

(You might want to read this before coming to group)

    Let's cut to the chase. We put this booklet together because we want people to experience a genuine encounter with God. Real people meeting our real God in a real way. A simple way.
    Let's start here: Who are you?

☐   A life-long "Christian"

☐   A good church-goer

☐   Someone who left "religion" behind after having it forced down my throat as a child

☐   A sincerely thinking person currently interested in checking out what *could be*

☐   I am a leader in the church, mature in my faith, and interested in engaging with God deeply as a way of life.

☐   I got dragged here and probably won't be back next time.

☐   None of the above. I'm more of: _____

_____

    Check a box, or make up your own (by the way, we're going to be writing in this book!). No matter what, we think **dtl** just might work for you.
    We believe that everyone is on a journey...finding what's worth living for. We've all looked, and are still looking, in many places that have left us unsatisfied. If we were honest with ourselves, it has even left us broken, wounded, maybe a bit confused, or just stale. Especially about who God is and how spiritual life works.

Religion provided a structure of sorts, and gave us a sense that we were all created to need an inner life connection to something larger than us. Some*One* larger than life. Still, it has left us thinking…

> "OK, wait. There's got to be something more than this. Most of the time I feel worse about myself and more distant from God. I thought 'church' or 'religion' would draw me closer, but I feel like I just can't reach Him."

We know ourselves too well, if we're not in denial. Perhaps you've heard this great definition of d-e-n-i-a-l—

"**d**on't **e**ven **n**otice **i** **a**m **l**ying."

Lying…to ourselves, or to others, it doesn't matter! Pretending, protecting our image, living according to the expectations of others, it all usually involves a little too much denial of reality.

But if you're looking for more; if you've decided it's time; if you are ready to care less about what people think, and you just want to grow in character and in closeness to God, then maybe this is a way we can get it done.

Some people in religious circles say,
"You have to live up to my standards, or go!"

On the other hand, God says,
"You can't possibly live up to my standards, so COME!"

That's the spirit of **dtl**. Come as you are. You get to be who you are, and talk about your current situation in your spiritual journey. Here's that place where you can finally ask those questions and express those opinions you thought would only serve up embarrassing rejection or unbearable conflict. Not here. It's safe here.

Call it a crossroads or a fork-in-the-road, you are about to decide if you want to see if God and real life intersect. Some have thought God only shows up in stain-glassed buildings. Others have concluded that God simply doesn't show up at all. Still others have limited their experience of God to pursuing information about God, conducting rituals about God, or doing good deeds for God.

Take the fork in the road that leads to discovering the life. Learn what it can be like to walk through life connected with God at the heart level as you live each moment.

We call this six-week tool a "reader" because when used in a group setting, it can be read straight through without comment. Think of it as a "curriculum" that teaches you how to be free from "curriculums." You are going to learn "4 Life-giving Practices" that you will be able to use the rest of your life no matter what group or study or class you might be participating in at the time. The Practices are designed to connect the deeper parts of who you are, the invisible and eternal parts of you, with our invisible and eternal God.

There are spots along the way ("stops" really), where you stop and talk some things over, offer your opinion, ask your questions, maybe write a few things down as a way to process your feelings and beliefs. We went ahead and marked them with our fork...

These "forks in the road" present the reader with an opportunity to go one direction or another. Sometimes, that direction needs to be down the same road, ignoring the fork. But sometimes the fork is your opportunity for new direction. You'll know in your heart.

So pretty much anyone can do this no matter what "level" of training or education or growth you've got under your belt. It doesn't matter. It's simple and self-explanatory. Of course it really gets good in the group setting when there are interruptions of the personal variety. Go ahead, shock your friends! Think out loud! You can let everyone else be in their process and better yet, let yourself be in yours!

Each week we'll read (and discuss) that week's chapter together out loud. No expectations to work ahead! No homework! Plan for about 90 minutes together. We'll read around the group circle, but you can always say, "Pass" if you don't feel like reading out loud.

Each week becomes progressively more discussion oriented by design. Less reading, more talking. You are always welcome to participate at whatever level you desire. You are in charge. We'll remind everyone in the group of that from time to time. Again, just say "pass" any time you don't want to do something out loud (read, share your thoughts, discuss, pray, whatever). Of course, you know that the more you "step out" and participate, the more you will get out of these times. Believe me, the old adage, "the only stupid question is the one that is not asked" is true in your **dtl** group! Go ahead...take a few risks! Here's the real key: what we do in **dtl** *doesn't* stay in **dtl**.

Let's clarify that. We value confidentiality and want to

cultivate trust so that people will feel increasingly free to share what's really going on inside. In that sense, what happens in **dtl** *stays* in **dtl**.

What we mean is that what we do in the group format needs to translate into real life. In other words everything we do in the group setting is better experienced during the other six days of the week when we are living normal life. That's the whole point. Give stuff a try every day. Mull over some things while you are standing in line, on hold, or in traffic. Create purposeful moments of rest with God. Do it with your spouse, kids, or other friends. Spend the week on the material you covered at group. It's all about practicing the four practices every day. We will never let you forget that life is really all about practice.

Anyway, your **dtl** coach will get the reading going, and then invite you to go around the circle reading a paragraph or so, whatever you are comfortable with. Before you know it you are into some interesting discussions. If you think you pretty much know everything that's being said, you are missing the point. Your opportunity is to bring a breath of fresh air to your personal experience with God. Strong people know that they never quit growing. If you think this stuff is as strange as it gets because the thoughts are so new, then your opportunity is to connect these new thoughts to your old set and discover the life they offer!

We're all on a journey of faith. For those who've travelled some distance, this is a six week course which will bring renewal if you let it. For others it will teach an approach to spiritual growth that frees us to read and understand the Bible for ourselves; brings Sunday sermons alive; and that can bring a new dimension of application to whatever "bible study" you have or will participate in.

Some are newer to this spiritual journey. What we have in common is that we are all discovering new and life-changing beliefs. The good news is that we all have the same opportunity and can walk along the road *together*! We can all become people able to find and experience the life-altering truth of God's Bible and apply it to the everyday moments of life!   And we all have something to offer each other along the way.

By the way, these six weeks of **dtl** are actually designed as an introduction to what we call "Life Groups." Life Groups are small groups of men or women that meet together weekly as a way of life. We've found that life works better when we isolate less and communicate more. It's our hope that six weeks from now you will have experienced enough of the benefits that you decide to make Life Group a way of life all your life.

Life is all about relationships when you think of it. So go ahead and stretch a bit. Take advantage of people who are at all different points of their spiritual journey. We are all discovering and living the story of our own lives! Let's share our stories together.

discover the life week #1:

life is really all about practice

We have something in common. We're all "finding what's worth living for." We're all on that same quest, aren't we? And it makes sense to do it together. It doesn't matter where we are on that journey, just that we want to grow as we go!

We are convinced that "finding what's worth living for" both begins and ends in a personal connection to the God who made us. Our goal, therefore, is to *experience* Him (rather than just know *about* Him), and to discover what He made us for! We do it all in the midst of every day life, bringing life and faith together in a real way. In order to accomplish that, we meet together weekly to learn and PRACTICE four "Life-giving PRACTICES" with the goal of PRACTICING them alone, and with our families and friends, all week long.

Though we hope everyone will decide to choose Life Group as a way of life all your life, we believe that embracing the four practices will change our lives, from the inside out, if we make it a lifestyle, with or without a Life Group.

What are the "4 Life-giving Practices"?

They are…
#1 - Life-giving Prayer: a way of communicating with God that is worshipful from start to finish, and potentially enjoyed with every breath we take!

#2 - Life-giving Truth: a simple way to discover what the Bible calls us to believe, followed by a commitment to practice believing it so that real life change takes place from the inside out.

#3 – Life-giving Relationships: An invitation to live a little more from the heart, being honest with yourself and others about what's really going on in there, embracing the hope that God Himself is able and willing to heal our brokenness as we seek Him together.

And
#4 - Life-giving Impact: discovering that bringing people together with the invisible and eternal is what's worth living for. So let's jump in…

PRACTICE #1...Life-giving Prayer

Life-giving Prayer is prayer for the purpose of *being with* God rather than *getting something from* God. This kind of prayer is focused on God (The King) and what He is doing (building His Kingdom) rather than on me and what I want Him to do for me!

Most often we find our prayers beginning with the words, "please," "thank you," and "I'm sorry." Those prayers are focused on me. The goal is to move beyond me and what I want and need to focus on God, what He's like, what He's done, and what He wants to do. It can be described as "worship without music."

We use the picture of perfect worship found in Revelation 4: 9 to help us understand what worship looks like. Here we see that worshipful prayer includes giving God **"Glory," "Honor"** and **"Thanks."** Let's talk about what those three things look like first, then we can talk about how to give God our needs in a worshipful way. Our goal is to make even that part of prayer worshipful!

1. To give God <u>glory</u>, we admire and adore Him:
   Giving God glory sounds like this:
   "God it's amazing that You are _____."
   "God, it's amazing that You are not _____."

Take a few moments to read through the "Phrases that give God glory" below. Get a feel for the words we might use in this kind of prayer. Go around the circle reading them out loud one at a time. If there is a blank, fill it in with one thing that comes to your mind. Read slowly so that everyone has a chance to connect with the words that are being said. The goal is not so much to connect our minds with facts about God as much as to connect our hearts to who He is and what it really means.

Phrases that give God glory:

- God, You are everywhere. No matter where I am, You are here!
- God, You are enough, it is true whether it feels like it or not.
- Almighty God, You are better than everyone and everything in life.
- Heavenly Father, You are self-existent, no one made You.
- You are self-sufficient, needing nothing from anyone to be complete.
- Father, You are huge. You hold the whole world in Your hands.
- God, You are mysterious, no one can understand You.
- God, You are the maker of everything.
- God, it's amazing that You are the God who knows everything and sees everything.

- God, You are creative, You imagined everything before You spoke it into place.
- God, You are infinite. You have no beginning and no end.
- You are all powerful, nothing can hinder or stop You.
- Father, You are in control, You always get what You choose.
- Father, You are glorious, I can't imagine the impact it will have on me to see You someday!
- God, You are unchanging, everyone else changes.
- You are faithful, everyone else will let me down.
- God, You are unlimited, everyone else is limited.
- Heavenly Father, You are forever, everyone else will die.
- God it is amazing that You are complete, everyone else is needy.
- God, You are unchanging in nature, even though we can't predict what You might do next.
- God, You are more beautiful than everything You have created.
- God, it's amazing that You are bigger than _____ .
- Father, I'm amazed that You are better than _____ .
- God, only You are able to _____ .
- God, You are not able to be threatened, overwhelmed, thwarted, intimidated, manipulated, predicted, controlled or overcome by anyone or anything!

stop & talk... Pick a phrase that stood out to you and tell the group why...

When we give God glory we simply consider what He is like. We're simply stating facts. We're not asking for anything. We're not even saying thanks. It's not about us and what He means to us, or how we feel about Him, it is just a choice to recognize who He is, and *wonder* at what that means. When we think about any aspect of who God is until it makes our hearts say, "Wow!" we have worshipped!

stop & talk... Discuss the impact on your life if you were more aware of who God is all day long. How would it change you if you made HIM (instead of you) the focus of your prayers?

2. To give God <u>honor</u>, we put Him above all things recognizing His profound majesty and absolute authority.

Giving God honor comes in two forms: 1) surrendering to God, and 2) choosing God over something else.

So, giving God honor through surrender sounds like this…

"God I really want _____,
   but I surrender it to you."
"God I really don't want _____,
   but I surrender it to You."

And, giving God honor by choosing Him sounds like this…

"God I choose You over _____."
"God, You are better than _____."

When we get in touch with the glory of God, giving Him honor is the only logical response. We honor Him when we surrender to Him, even when it doesn't feel good. We honor Him when we choose Him over everything else that we love and want.

Again, take time to read slowly through "Phrases that give God honor." And remember, there are many words we can use to give God honor, but the heart of this practice is choosing God *over* the things that we want and love and surrendering *to* God in situations that are hard or un-wanted.

Phrases that give God honor:

- God I surrender to You in _____.
- God I choose You over _____.
- I choose you over _____ (name someone you care for).
- I choose you over _____ (name something you love).
- God I surrender _____ to you. (a difficulty you are facing).
- God I surrender _____ to you (a person you are concerned about).
- God I choose You right now. You are better.
- You are God and I surrender to You.
- You can do whatever you want to with my life.
- I *want* You to do whatever You want with my life.
- I surrender my _____ (Go ahead and read through this list: children, marriage, job, addictions, health, relationships, church, plans, habits, dreams, goals, ambitions, etc.)
- Okay, God!   (if you think about it, this really sums it all up.)
- No matter what happens I'll be okay because I have YOU and You are enough.

- It's good if I don't get what I want because YOU are better than anything I may want.
- I don't have to be happy now, this isn't my life. My real life is in heaven.
- I surrender to this season of sickness You have designed for me.
- I choose Your will over my comfort.
- I choose to be content with loneliness, because You are enough, and better than people.
- I choose to worship You.
- I need You, want You, trust You, I'm Yours...It's all about You!

stop & talk... Discuss the impact it might have on your life if you chose to make those kinds of declarations to God throughout each day.

The reality is that we rarely *feel* like God is better than our family, friends, health, dreams, goals, work, reputation, etc. And it doesn't mean we stop working to reach for or enjoy those things. It simply means that we learn to believe and remember that we can't build our lives upon these things.

God knows that as visual people, visible things will more often *feel* better to us. We are exercising our will away from living for things, to serving God. We **know** that He **is** better, simply because He is not weak, needy, or temporary like everything else that He created. He can be trusted, while nothing else can. He is the ultimate authority. It makes sense to surrender to Him.

When we choose Him it teaches our hearts to *enjoy* things and *love* people, but ***worship*** only Him.

When we surrender to Him, we are simply expressing our willingness to let Him be God of every detail of our lives. We invite Him to do whatever He wants to with our lives because He is God and we are not! The more specific we are as we submit, the more powerful it will be in our lives.

Having considered God's glory, and then purposefully surrendering our hearts to Him, we find ourselves ready to offer thanksgiving for the things in life that really matter. As we make Life-giving Prayer a way of life, our eyes are beginning to see the world differently than ever before. Let's learn a new way of giving thanks to God...

3. To give God <u>thanks</u> in a worshipful way, we focus our thanks on the reality that the God of the universe cares about us.

Read through the following phrases slowly. Every human being on planet earth can give thanks for these things right now, no matter what:

- Your love for me is perfect.
- You created me and sustain my life every day.
- There is nothing I can do to make You love me more.
- There is nothing I can do to make You love me less.
- You don't need me for anything, but You still want me.
- God, you are not just everywhere, you are with me.
- You know everything about me.
- You sent Jesus to die in my place.

Did you notice the significance of these things? Especially the last phrase? The Bible has revealed that we find life on earth and for eternity by admitting our need for a Savior. That Savior is Jesus.

For those who have surrendered to God by placing their faith in Jesus' death on the cross in their place, we will have thanksgivings galore! So for all who have trusted Jesus as their Savior…

Giving God thanks sounds like this:
"Jesus, because You died for me I am _____."
"Jesus, because You died for me I have _____."
"Jesus, because You died for me I can _____."

Phrases that give God thanks:

- Jesus, because you died for me I am a new person.
- Because of Jesus I have your Spirit living in me.
- Jesus, because you died for me I can live forever in heaven.
- Because of Jesus I am perfect to You right now and always!
- Jesus, you gave me every spiritual blessing in the heavenly places.
- Jesus, because you died for me I can live for you!
- Jesus I have your power to say "No" to temptation.
- Because of Jesus You need nothing from me.
- Jesus, because you died for me I have Your power inside of me.
- Jesus, because you died for me I don't have to perform for You.
- Because you died for me I get to go to heaven for sure!
- Thanks that this life is not all there is.

- You are still at work in me, and You want to use me!
- Jesus when You died it was for every sin that I will ever commit.
- I celebrate that my sin is forgiven, and I will never be condemned.
- I am so thankful that my guilt and shame are gone!
- Thanks that I am Yours!
- I love that You always know what is best.
- Thanks that You always do what is best.
- You will be faithful to me even when I'm unfaithful.
- Jesus, there is nothing I can DO to UNDO what You DID on the cross!
- God, thank you that I am always beautiful to You because I am dressed in Jesus!
- Jesus, I love You. (perhaps the best way to say "thank you")

stop & talk... Discuss the impact it had on you to read those phrases. Pick one and talk about why it stood out to you.

Let's keep our conversation real here: there may be things on that list that you don't understand or even believe. That's okay. You can focus on the ones that do connect with your heart and we can process the others together later. The main thing for right now is to understand that when we give thanks to God we want it to be a celebration of all that He means to our hearts!

What is unique about this practice is our intentional effort at giving thanks for what is invisible and eternal. While it is good to give thanks for physical blessings, it is vital that we not focus on them. Things like food, clothing, shelter, health, jobs, finances, success, safety, or even our closest relationships. Those are the very things we are tempted to worship. We put our hope in having them. We think we can't live without them.

That's why whenever we say thanks for tangible things, we must learn to immediately remind ourselves that if God takes them all away we'll be okay because our lives are built on Jesus, not any of His gifts. Then, if we purposefully celebrate what His person means to our hearts it will keep us from worshipping His blessings on our lives and teach us to worship Him. We practice giving thanks for the invisible things because we know that they last forever and are the only things that can satisfy our hearts.

So let's step up to the challenge of learning how to be thankful in prayer for those things God most enjoys giving to us, knowing that it is those things that most bless us! It is not the graces of this world that will bring us fulfillment, but instead we're told...

> *Fix your hope **completely**
> on the grace that is to be revealed
> at the revelation of Jesus Christ!"*
> - 1 Peter 1:13 -

4. To give God our <u>needs</u>, means that we come to Him as the source of all things, knowing He knows best.

When we think of prayer, we most often think of making requests. Even these prayers can be worshipful if we come recognizing our dependence on Him. Focusing on what HE wants to accomplish rather than on what we want Him to do for us *is* worship.

The invisible Holy Spirit is always working to fulfill the kingdom of God. Focusing our prayers on His work in people, through trial and tragedy, makes our requests life-giving. We'll stay connected to the only thing that matters, the only thing worth living for! We're not going to ask God to fix what we *think* is *wrong* in our lives and the lives of those we love anymore. Instead, we ask Him to use every circumstance to accomplish His purposes in us and to draw others to Himself *through* them, as hard as it may be.

Giving God our needs sounds like this:
"*Holy Spirit, use _____ for Your purposes."*
"*God, please work in our hearts while this is happening."*

Let's read through "Phrases that give God our needs" in the same way we have done before.

Phrases that give God our needs:

- Holy Spirit, use this conflict to have Your way in each person involved.
- God, please have Your way in this illness.
- God, establish Your rule in our hearts through this trial.
- God, please use this evil to accomplish Your good purposes.
- Father, please comfort the grieving, and use this death to draw people around it to Yourself.
- Holy Spirit, have Your way in my son at school today.
- Holy Spirit, work in my husband as he faces this trial.

- Holy Spirit, in the midst of the pain allow my friend to experience You.
- Father, work in my heart while I'm being betrayed by my friend.
- God, work mightily to reveal Yourself in this difficulty.
- God, I want you to use this unfair coach in my child's life.
- God, please teach me to trust You during this financial struggle.
- God, will you use our presence at this ball game to draw people to Yourself?
- God, let the truth that You are in control override my fears about how my kids turn out.
- God, let Your glory captivate my heart so that I don't worship my family instead of You.
- God, please give me passion for Your kingdom that is greater than my passion for this life.
- God, help me to see my money, time, health, home, family, job, activities, etc. as mostly about helping people find Jesus.
- Holy Spirit, please remind me today that my real purpose for going to work is bigger than my work. It's about Your work!

stop & talk... What impact would it have if you practiced focusing your requests on what God wants rather than on what you want?

Hopefully you are beginning to get a sense of why we are working at learning to pray in this new way. Life-giving prayers are prayers that connect our hearts with who God is and what He has done. Life is to be found under Him. In that humble, God-centered place we teach our hearts what matters most. It has the power to change us from the inside out and give us life.

Each week we will practice Life-giving Prayer on our own throughout the week. At **dtl** we are learning how all this works and feels. We're getting used to the idea of talking out loud with each other about our experiences during the week so that we can encourage and learn from each other. After telling our stories we will experience a time of worship together! Try it on your own this week, and we'll do it together next week.

PRACTICE #2...Life-giving Truth

Life-giving Truth is the practice of telling ourselves God's truth over and over again so that it sinks into our hearts and changes us from the inside out.

As we read the Bible we learn to ask one very important question, "What is this passage calling me to believe?" We practice taking the focus off of the instructions of God and put it onto the truth of God. It is only when we believe what God says is true that we will be freed to live out His instructions. We learn not to focus on the information that we can add to our storehouse of knowledge, OR on the behavioral demands that can make us look better on the outside and feel better on the inside. Instead, we're changing our heart beliefs and finding the freedom God promises us in John 8:32,

"You will know the truth and the truth will make you free."

It is *not* when our *minds* grasp a truth that it changes us. That's just the first step. When finally our *hearts* grasp it, then we have been changed from the inside out. When we choose to live in a truth, repeating it over and over again and connecting it with the everyday moments of life, our hearts will grasp it. Its power will become evident as it changes us! It is exactly what the Bible is talking about...

Proverbs 3:1-3
*My son, do not forget my teaching,
but let your **heart** keep my commandments;
for length of days and years of life and peace they will add to you.
Do not let kindness and truth leave you;
bind them around your neck, <u>**write them on the tablet of your heart**</u>.*

For example, let's take a look at one of the most famous verses in the Bible, John 3:16...

"For <u>God so loved the world</u> that <u>He gave His only begotten Son</u>, that whoever believes in Him <u>shall not perish, but have eternal life</u>."

There is a lot of Life-giving Truth in this one verse. Look at the underlined words and discuss their implications.

stop & talk...

What does the first underlined phrase tell us about ourselves?

What does the second underlined phrase reveal about God?

And what does the third underlined phrase reveal about life?

Many of us are familiar with the words *"For God so loved the world."* Yet how many of us have really taken to heart the truth about how loved we are so that it affects who we are every single day? Let's work toward that this week.
Try telling yourself this truth all day long,

"I am SO loved."

Say it when you wake up and before you fall asleep. Say it when you feel like a success and when you feel like a failure. Remind yourself that it has nothing to do with either! Tell your kids about how much God loves you, and them, and invite them to remind you that you are SO loved by Him. Just say it randomly to yourself out loud or to someone else,

"God loves you SO much!"

Next week we will share whether or not we remembered to think about the truth and how it affected our hearts and lives if we did. We will then discuss a new truth and consider the ways it would change our lives if we took it to heart all week long. That will become our pattern!

PRACTICE #3...Life-giving Relationships

Life-giving Relationships gives us the chance to be real with each other about what is going on inside of us. It's not easy since much of it is not very pretty. Being honest and genuine about "hidden" things, though, is a freeing and powerful choice. It is so much more life-giving than our other option: pretending we're something that we're not.

Before you get scared off, know that no one will ever put pressure on you to share anything about yourself that you don't want to share. You never have to do anything you don't want to do. We will give you lots of invitations, but you don't have to share until you are ready!

The reality is that much of what is going on inside of us is blocking our connection with God. This blockage is keeping us from experiencing the joy and life He offers. If we could fix it ourselves we would. But we can't. We've tried. And then we tried even harder.

The choice is ours to keep hiding, or share honestly for the purpose of healing in the context of real relationships. Our hope is in God's promise to work in us through prayer.

When someone has shared honestly we refrain from giving advice. We don't judge, and we don't minimize it. Since we're looking for real change from the inside out rather than behavioral modification, we choose to pray instead. We're not talking about "self-help" here, we're calling on God, in the name of Jesus Christ!

We ask God to work deeply inside of our friend. Only He can fix what is wrong. In the context of Life-giving Relationships, we not only experience the power of real and gracious relationships, but we experience God's power changing us from the inside out.

By the way, we don't have to share the circumstances or the details connected to what is going on inside of us. For instance, if I am angry, I don't have to explain *who* or *what* made me angry in order for you to pray for God to heal my angry spirit. That keeps me from taking up the whole group time with too many details. Even better, it keeps me from talking about others in a negative way. The door for gossip never opens when we limit our words to what is going on in our own heart.

Life-giving Relationships invites us to decide that changing and growing is more important than "making a good impression," or keeping up a good image.

Each week we'll have the chance to share with each other how we sense God is working inside of us and to ask for prayer!

PRACTICE #4...Life-giving Impact

Life-giving Impact is discovering the thrill of giving others the gift of Jesus by praying a simple prayer as we go about our daily lives. We can offer people the life we have found in a quiet and unobtrusive way by cultivating a "Pray & Watch" lifestyle. We pray the following prayer for everyone and then watch for the Holy Spirit at work in their hearts.

We've come to call it "The 5-second prayer":

> *"Holy Spirit, draw the heart of this person to Yourself and make him a kingdom laborer!"*

Life-giving Impact is based on the belief that what everyone on this planet needs most is an ever-deepening connection with the one true God which can only be found in Jesus Christ.

Acts 4:12
And there is salvation in no one else; for there is no other name under heaven that has been given among men by which we must be saved.

It's only through the name of Jesus. But people can only receive the truth about Jesus by the work of God's Spirit inside of them, drawing them to Himself. Jesus said, in...

John 6:44
No one can come to Me unless the Father who sent Me draws him.

God doesn't ask us to persuade people or change people, and He doesn't need us to perform for Him. He invites us to pray that His Spirit will do the work inside of people drawing their hearts to Him *and* give them a passion for others to know Him, becoming laborers for His kingdom building...

Matthew 9:36-38
<u>**Ask**</u> *the Lord of the harvest to send workers into His harvest.*

This kind of prayer includes us in the miracles and thrills connected to the lost being found as it is described in Luke 15.

Each of us will form a "Pray&Watch List." We put people on the list with whom we are in contact on a regular basis. We are not sure that they have connected with God in a personal way. We're not deciding where they are, and neither are we judging anyone. We're just giving them an incredible gift: God's work within them to bring more life than they are experiencing now!

Perhaps our friend has stagnated in her growth with God. Maybe he lacks a sense of vision and purpose for his life. Perhaps they lack certainty that they are going to heaven. In some cases, we know people who are strongly disbelieving and even angry toward organized religion, people who have been poor examples of God's love, and even God Himself. In any case, we pray, and we can pray anytime day or night and every day of the week, for everyone on our list, when we see them, think of them, or are praying through our list.

At Life Group we tell stories of how God is working in us and through us as we pray. Then we will pray together in this way:

The Life Group coach prays "The 5 Second Prayer," followed by every group member saying the first names of all the people on their lists, all at the same time, out loud. In a very short time we pray for scores, even hundreds! It is the most significant request we could ask of our God who longs to save souls and send laborers into His kingdom!

Some "wrap-up" questions after week #1...

Life Group offers us a great opportunity to share about real, current, and personal things, but we want you to feel no pressure at all. Be yourself, take your time, and speak your mind, but always feel free to say "I'll pass" if you want to! So...

1) Do you have any questions about the 4 Life-giving Practices?

2) Which of the 4 practices is most interesting to you personally? Why?

discover the life week #2:

life is really all about practice

Before we talk about how our first week with the 4 Life-giving Practices went, let's think down the line a ways. After "Discover the Life" is done, you'll have the chance to join a "Life Group" where…

…We share about and experience all four Life-giving Practices every time the group gathers.

…We are all encouraged to invite new people to the group at any time.

…The group will multiply and become two groups whenever it grows past six people. We won't feel like we want to, but we commit to multiplying anyway because the "Life-giving Lifestyle" is too good to keep to ourselves!

…Each person determines the impact of Life Group on their own lives by how much they invest throughout the week.

…There is no end date for the group, but anyone is free to stop coming, switch to a new group, attend more than one group, or start a new group at any time.

… So why not start thinking about it now, "Who do you know that might enjoy Life Group?"

PRACTICE #1…Life-giving Prayer

Last week we defined Life-giving Prayer as "prayer that is more about being **with** God than getting something **from** God." Let's take a look at Psalm 131:2 to better understand what that means:

Surely I have composed and quieted my soul;
like a weaned child rests against his mother,
my soul is like a weaned child within me.

When a *nursing* child comes to his mother he is coming with a demanding spirit. He is aware of his need and wants to have it met…now! Give that child 200 more pounds and his energy would be lethal!

On the other hand, when a *weaned* child comes to his mother, it is merely to connect with her person. He wants to be with her, connecting his heart with her heart until he feels ready to get down and go on with life. Often it is when he is hurt, scared, sad or lonely and just needs his mother's presence, love, and reassurance. Other times it is just because it feels good to be with her. Sometimes he just wants to show her that he cares about her and loves her! The love of a weaned child is maturing and becoming more and more mutual…less selfish.

That describes so perfectly what Life-giving Prayer is all about! **Let's review** the four kinds of Life-giving Prayer so that we can practice them together today:

Giving God glory:
"God it is amazing that You are_____."
"God, it is amazing that You are not_____."

Giving God honor:
"God I surrender _____ to you."
"God I choose you over _____."

Giving God thanks:
"Jesus, because You died for me I am _____."
"Jesus, because You died for me I have _____."
"Jesus, because You died for me I can _____."

Giving God our needs:
"Holy Spirit, use _____ for Your purposes."
"God, please work in our hearts while this is happening."

As you prepare to worship:
We're going to keep this prayer time very simple by just using the phrases above. Simply choose a statement and then fill in the blank with your own words.

Consider praying out loud even if you never have before. It is easier to begin this way because it is short and some of the words have been chosen for you. It is genuine and personal because you fill in the blanks with what is real to you. Please don't worry about your words. The best prayer is the real one! In fact, if you need more help, turn back to pages 10-17 and use some of the full phrases we printed there.

If you've done a lot of group praying, this might feel a bit stiff to you. You might be tempted to wander away from this format. You might find yourself using words and patterns of prayer that have become habits over the years. Again, let's work at forging a little new territory!

Please work at staying focused. We are learning how to give God glory, honor, thanks, and our needs in a way that is, perhaps, different than we've done before. We're all learning! Remember, *discovering* is all about putting the old in the rear-view mirror, and, by faith, stretching out to a horizon filled with something new!

It is worth the awkwardness of "re-learning" to pray. Remember, we're just practicing. Life is really all about practice! There is no need to feel concerned about what we say. And don't feel awkward about silence. Silence is a good thing.

Your **dtl** coach will transition you from one section to the next until we've experienced all four: first glory, then honor, then thanks, and finally needs. Again, just use the phrases on the last page and simply fill in the blanks with your relevant thoughts.

stop & pray... Spend a few moments in Life-giving Prayer together.

stop & talk... Now talk about how it felt to pray this way. Was it awkward for you? Did you sense how good this could be?

Remember that new things never feel comfortable, especially in comparison to what you're used to. In time you will become more familiar with Life-giving Prayer and experience the benefits of the hard work!

Here's an idea for you to try:

Pray in this same way all week long. Do it out loud whenever you can. As you hear yourself pray it heightens your awareness that God is actually with you and you are talking to Him. It also helps those of us who are not used to praying out loud in a group. We become more comfortable with hearing our own voices in prayer.

The goal is to use the moments throughout the day to connect with God. Anytime we don't have to be focused on something else is the right time! We are training ourselves to see all of the circumstances of life as opportunities to see God, communicate with Him, and participate in the work God is doing.

We have to be purposeful about connecting with God, because we are distracted and our minds need to be retrained to take advantage of each opportunity. We have to be purposeful about first giving Him glory, honor and thanks, because we naturally think "God gimme!" We have to re-train ourselves to request what God wants because we are so in touch with what we want! God is invisible and we are often attentive only to the visible. If we refocus and re-train, our prayers will become life-giving. As they become our lifestyle we'll experience their life changing power!

Remember, this is not a duty. It is an incredible opportunity! Whenever we miss out on one, another immediately follows it! Next time we will begin by sharing with each other whether or not we remembered to worship God and how it impacted our hearts! Every breath is an opportunity to praise Him!

PRACTICE #2...Life-giving Truth

Last week we defined Life-giving Truth as principles from God's word to believe. Truths that have the power to change us from the inside out if we take them to heart. In Life Group we identify and discuss a Life-giving Truth and then leave with the goal to tell that truth to ourselves over and over again throughout the week, connecting it to the everyday moments of our life.

It's not so much our overall belief system that dictates our behaviors and attitudes in a given moment. It is what our heart truly believes about the specifics of that moment.

Remember the Life-giving Truth from Week #1?
"I am SO loved by God"

stop & talk... How did you do with telling yourself that truth during the everyday moments of life? Did it have an impact on your heart? Do you really believe it yet?

Now, for this week's truth...

Read Psalm 139:7-10 and look for the Life-giving Truth.

Where can I go from Your Spirit? Or where can I flee from Your presence? If I ascend to heaven, You are there; if I make my bed in Sheol, behold, You are there. If I take the wings of the dawn, if I dwell in the remotest part of the sea, even there Your hand will lead me, and Your right hand will lay hold of me.

stop & talk...How would you summarize the truth we are invited to believe from Psalm 139:7-10?

Now, consider these thoughts together:

God is everywhere. There is nowhere I can go to get away from Him. It is true, whether or not I feel it, believe it, or care about it! But it will only change my life if I choose to make myself continually aware of it! When my heart believes it, even unconsciously, I'm changed!

A great summary truth from these verses is this: **God is here**. We're going to tell ourselves this truth all week. Let's consider this phrase in three different ways:

<u>**GOD**</u> is here.

God <u>**IS**</u> here.

God is <u>**HERE**</u>.

stop & talk... Talk about the slightly different implications of each of these three phrases.

Remember, no matter how you say it, or how often, it won't really impact your life unless you let it connect with your heart!

stop & talk... How do you think it would affect your life if you were more aware of the fact that GOD IS HERE, during each and every moment of your daily life?

This is a truth everyone knows, and most people "believe," but it's not changing our life if our heart doesn't really embrace it or is consistently distracted from it.

Next week we will start our Life-giving Truth time by sharing how it affected our hearts and lives during the week. Remember that this is not an obligation but an opportunity. You aren't doing this to impress God or anyone here. Instead simply expect to experience the power and change of Life-giving Truth! Here are five suggestions for ways to train your mind to think about the truth:

1) Ask a friend or a family member to do it with you and help you to remember.

2) Write it on sticky notes and put them where you'll see them.

3) Connect it with a certain activity you do all day long:
   ➤ Every time you get in the car.
   ➤ Every time you take a drink of something.

4) Set a cell phone alarm to go off throughout the day to remind you.

5) Hang a white board or chalk board in a prominent place at home and write the truth of the week on it. Everyone can see and be reminded all day!

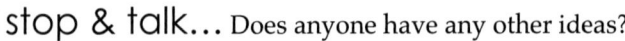

stop & talk... Does anyone have any other ideas?

PRACTICE #3...Life-giving Relationships

As we consider, again, the idea of being real with each other, and about living life openly and honestly, let's take a look at what God has to say about it. Let's read James 5:13-18...

13 Is anyone among you suffering? Then he must pray. Is anyone cheerful? He is to sing praises.
14 Is anyone among you sick? Then he must call for the elders of the church and they are to pray over him, anointing him with oil in the name of the Lord;
15 and the prayer offered in faith will restore the one who is sick, and the Lord will raise him up, and if he has committed sins, they will be forgiven him.
16 Therefore, confess your sins to one another, and pray for one another so that you may be healed. *The effective prayer of a righteous man can accomplish much.*
17 Elijah was a man with a nature like ours, and he prayed earnestly that it would not rain, and it did not rain on the earth for three years and six months.
18 Then he prayed again, and the sky poured rain and the earth produced its fruit.

Verse 16 is our key verse, but the context is important to our understanding. Look back now at verses 13 and 14. They are a call to be real about our circumstances and heart. Notice that verse 15 is an invitation for us to ask church leaders to pray for us when we are physically sick. Verse 16 is an invitation to confess what is really going on in our hearts, not for forgiveness, but for healing. We confess to God for forgiveness (1 John 1:9). We confess to each other because being real is better than appearing perfect. Confession is good for the soul, right? And we "confess" so that another will pray for us so that we may be healed. Healing. That's what we're after here.

stop & talk... Why is it so much easier to be real about <u>physical</u> problems than it is to be real about <u>spiritual</u> problems?

Now take a look at the following statements connected to the verses after verse 16. If you were to read the original account of this event in 1 Kings 17 and 18, you'll see that…

1. Elijah was just like you are…a flawed human.

2. God told Him to pray that it wouldn't rain, so he did. It didn't rain for 42 months.

3. God didn't NEED Elijah to pray, but wanted Him to be part of this miracle.

4. The request Elijah made was not his idea, but God's.

Here's the point: ***We can be a part of the miracle of God healing the deep and broken places of each other's hearts.***

It takes two ingredients: 1) One flawed person talks about what's broken in his own heart, and 2) Another flawed person asks Jesus to heal that broken part in his friend's heart.
Could it be simpler? Yet promise so much life?
Imagine what we miss when we hide what is wrong instead of confessing it! Remember, I'm not confessing a "sin" so that I can be forgiven. I'm identifying something broken inside that makes me sin, and asking you to ask Jesus to fix what I can't fix.
So rather than telling you that I was jealous several times this week, I can let you in on the fact that jealousy controls my heart. I don't know where it comes from or how to get rid of it, but I hate it.
I don't need to share any more than that. I don't need you to hammer me for it, or to tell me it's no big deal. I don't need your advice. I just need you to understand, accept me, and pray that God would heal whatever is broken that makes me jealous!
By the way, when a person asks for healing prayer, we like to gather around them to show our support. We might lay a hand on their shoulder or knee or foot to symbolize that though I can only touch you this far, God is touching you at the heart. It is a cool illustration of us being in it together, totally dependent on God. But we leave that all up to the person we are praying for and what they are comfortable with.

stop & talk & pray… Does anyone have something in their lives that they can't seem to overcome? Who wants to be healed from the inside out? Would you like us to pray for you?

You will be given this opportunity every week. It might seem kind of strange, and that's ok. On the other hand, it just might be the coolest thing you've ever experienced!

No one will ever push you to share until you are comfortable and it is your idea! You are in complete control of if, when, and what you choose to share! And you get to decide whether or not anyone lays hands on you! Once again, it is not an obligation or expectation, just an opportunity.

PRACTICE #4...Life-giving Impact

Review the "Pray&Watch" 5-second prayer...

"Holy Spirit, please work in the heart of _____ to draw him to yourself and make him a kingdom laborer."

We're making a lifestyle of praying that 5-second prayer. The first part of the prayer is vital. Nothing is more important in life than a person trusting Jesus Christ as Savior, surrendering fully to Him as Lord. We are ready to really live only if we are truly ready to die! Our heart has discovered that total surrender to Jesus as Lord *is* life!

The second half of the 5-second prayer is very important because we want the good news to spread to the whole world. When someone comes to know Jesus, we want them to care about others knowing Him too. Then they will pray for people.

When we all pray for the people we know, the impact will go on and on and on! That's what it means to "be a kingdom laborer." We pray because we believe the most important thing for everyone on the planet is that they figure out where they stand with God. We don't want to be intrusive, but we really care so we choose to "pray" and then "watch" what God does.

stop & write... Think of the first names of 10 or more people. The more the better. Add to it day by day. You can start your list right here and continue on the next page...

_____   _____

_____   _____

_____   _____

_____   _____

_____

We're after a lifestyle of praying rather than a once-a-day activity. As we look out the window at our neighbor's house or walk past the desk of a co-worker, we utter the 5-second prayer.

Also, we take a couple of minutes somewhere in our day, like in the car on the way to work, or as we fall into bed, to pray for everyone on our list, and everyone we happen to think of in the moment!

When we find ourselves praying for people we don't even know, at the grocery store, in a restaurant, at school, in traffic, in the jet flying overhead, we'll know that God is changing our heart and mindset about what matters most in life. When our first response is to pray instead of getting annoyed or angry we'll know that God is actually changing us from the inside out!

Pray&Watch is based on the invisible work of God's Spirit in the hearts of people. That is our only hope of finding what's worth living for…more of Jesus in my life <u>and</u> the opportunity to be involved in helping others find Him.

stop & pray… Now Pray&Watch together.

Next week we will have an opportunity to share how Pray&Watch affected us during the week, and to share anything we noticed while we "watched" God at work in the lives of others!

To end our time together, and as a way to get to know each other, share a little bit about your spiritual journey by answering the following two questions.

stop & talk... Have you invited Jesus to be your personal Lord and Savior? If so, when and how?

What kind of spiritual growth are you interested in right now?

If you have not yet given your life to Christ or are unsure about how that works, please feel free to process out loud with the group. Or, you could grab your coach afterward and talk. We want this to be a safe place where anyone can express their thoughts and ASK ANY QUESTION WHATSOEVER without feeling any embarrassment or pressure.

Enjoy your week with God and the 4 Life-giving Practices!

discover the life week #3:

Life is really all about practice

PRACTICE #1...Life-giving Prayer

Before we share with each other about our first week with the practices, we need to remind ourselves that this it is not a duty or an obligation, just an opportunity. It is normal to forget. We have to retrain our minds to think about God *as we are living.* That takes diligence and time. Don't feel guilty about forgetting...ever!

When we don't remember to worship God, we can celebrate that He doesn't *need* us to worship Him! He knows who He is. This is not an exercise to increase God's self esteem! When we forget to take advantage of the opportunity to worship Him "breath by breath" we can celebrate that His love for us is not at all affected by our performance, good OR bad! He is not more pleased with us if we do worship Him. Nor is He less pleased with us if we don't.

The truth is that the only reason we are in any way pleasing to God is because of Jesus' death and resurrection and His drawing us to Himself, making us His child. It's all about His performance on our behalf! Our performance means nothing to Him!

With that in mind it is safe for us to ask each other...

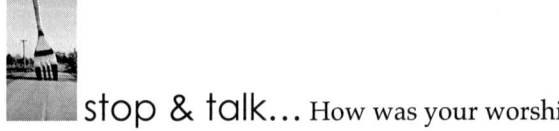 stop & talk... How was your worship of God this week?

Did you remember to do it?

Did it have an impact on your heart?"

What about God made your heart say wow?

Before we actually experience some Life-giving Prayer together, consider all the ways to fill in this blank,

"God, only You _____."

We want to introduce a variety of ways to express glory to God, since our God's many attributes are beyond comprehension! He alone is worthy of worship and it is important to connect His worthiness with…

...giving Him glory (praising Him):
God, *only You <u>created the world</u>*

...giving Him honor (surrendering to Him):
God, *only You <u>are in complete control of the world and me</u>*

...giving Him thanks (for the invisible and eternal):
God, *only You <u>have ultimate victory over death and hell</u>*

...giving Him our needs (making our requests life-giving):
God, *only You <u>know what I really need in this situation</u>*

It helps our hearts to learn that He alone is worthy of our worship. It takes us down the path of becoming a walking worshipper.

During this prayer time we'll fill in the blanks again, with a small change as noted below. Your coach will still transition the group as we go. Here are the sentences we will use…

Giving God glory…
*I praise You because **only You** are _____.*
*Wow, God, it's amazing that **only You** can _____.*

Giving God honor…
*I surrender _____ to You because **only You** _____.*
*I choose You over _____ because **only You** _____.*

Giving God thanks…
*I love You because **only You** _____.*

Giving God our needs…
*I seek Your will in _____ because **only You** _____.*

stop & pray… Now let's practice worshipping God.

After prayer:
What did you experience during the prayer time? Feel free to express frustrations, discomfort, general weirdness, whatever! We're learning together and it will be that much more meaningful if we let each other know how we feel each week!

 stop & talk... Take a moment to talk about how that felt.

PRACTICE #2...Life-giving Truth

Let's share about how last week's truth "God is here," affected our lives. Don't forget: this is not a performance. Don't feel pressure or guilt if you totally forgot. Don't feel pride if you remembered! If we told ourselves the truth even *one time* this week, that's great! That is something to build on. If we didn't, that's okay. Each moment provides a new opportunity to try again!

stop & talk... Talk about how the idea that "God is here" impacted your week.

Now let's discover a new truth about God for this week. Here is just one of many verses that reveal it:

The Lord is my shepherd I shall not want.
- Psalm 23:1 -

Read each of the following possible summaries of Psalm 23:1:

#1 God is so amazing I **shouldn't** want anything but Him.

#2 God is so amazing I **don't** want anything but Him.

#3 God is so amazing that I **can be** content without anything but Him.

stop & talk... As a group talk about which one of those phrases seems like the best way to understand those verses.

Now consider this:
If statement #1 is the correct understanding, where would that take us? Whether or not we *should* want other things, we do, right? And we probably always will! Approaching our spiritual lives with the word *"should"* only leads to guilt and shame. It often motivates us to avoid rather than to jump in and discover.

In the same way, most of us would admit that we could not honestly say statement #2, "I *don't* ever want anything but God." We know our hearts too well. We would be lying, at least to ourselves, if we didn't admit that often what we want is God and a little something else.

Now notice that statement #3 is simply true all the time. The power of Life-giving Truth is that we can choose to say it at any time, even when we don't feel it. Even if we're struggling to believe it! If it is true sometimes, it is true all the time. That's why we're after the *truth* in the Bible. It is true because He created me in His image and for fellowship with Him. It is simply a fact...

God, all by Himself, is enough for me!

He always has been <u>and</u> He always will be. I'll never want or need anything that He can't provide for me in Himself.
This truth,
GOD IS ENOUGH,
is the reason we can be content in the middle of anything. We can have courage to face anything. This truth is where we put all of our hope!

We don't know what God will give us, or withhold from us. We don't and can't know what God will do. We only know that He will always be enough to completely satisfy our hearts in the middle of anything life dishes out!

stop & talk... How do you think it would affect you if you chose to believe this truth in the everyday moments of your life?

Let's try it this week and see!

PRACTICE #3...Life-giving Relationships

Before we share about how God worked through our time of healing prayer from last week, let's remind ourselves again of what is true.

It is not our job to heal ourselves. We can't heal each other. So there is no pressure on us to "fix," or "be fixed." Yes, the group prayed for us, but God is still in charge. Neither the group, nor any group member who is prayed for, needs to feel like a failure if there is no evidence of change.

When we ask how our week went after being prayed for, we can be totally honest. Sometimes healing happens in a very powerful, instant way. Most often it is a process and we don't know what it will look like or how long it will take. God's timing is perfect. Sometimes it is time God uses to heal us. Sometimes the issue seems to get even worse before it gets better. We aren't in charge of when or how God works, we just pray, surrender, and choose to believe that God is doing it. We're learning to live by faith. We can keep praying for each other all the way through that process. All we have to do is ask!

stop & talk & pray... Does anyone have something going on inside of them that they would like prayer for this week?

PRACTICE #4…Life-giving Impact

As you share how Pray&Watch went this week, remember that it is a brand new habit and will take time to catch on. If anyone remembered to pray "The 5-Second Prayer," listen to them share about how it affected them. Ask your **dtl** coach to share how this lifestyle has impacted his/her heart.

 stop & talk… Now share Pray&Watch stories.

Before you Pray&Watch together, think a minute about the "watch" part.

"Watching" is active, not passive. The more closely we can connect our lives with a person on our Pray&Watch list, the better view we will have when the miracle unfolds! We'll see God in ways we never have before. He'll become more real to us than He has ever been. We will see our hearts changing, and our relationships growing. Best of all, we'll have the thrill of "watching" the often small steps of change in other's lives. God is drawing people to Himself all the time. You've experienced it in your own life, right? Perhaps before you were aware of it! We can experience the joy of having been part of the miracle!

"Watching" can be thought of as *"being around people with anticipation."* The more we are around people anticipating God's work the more we will see God working!

We want to continually add new people to our Pray&Watch list. Have you found that you are noticing people more? The more people we bring before God the more miracles we will watch. See if you can remember the names you wrote down last week. Write them down again (it will help you remember them when the list isn't in front of you). Then add some new names…

_____   _____

_____   _____

_____ _____

_____ _____

_____ _____

_____ _____

_____ _____

_____ _____

_____ _____

*"Holy Spirit please work in the hearts of these people.
Draw them to yourself
and fill them with passion for others to know You too."*

 stop & pray... Now Pray&Watch together.

By the way, have you noticed that we've phrased the 5-Second Prayer slightly differently each time? We don't want anyone thinking this is a "magic prayer," or that the words themselves are what matter. The important thing is that we ask for two things: 1) God to draw people's hearts to Jesus, and 2) That they not only come to faith, but that when they do, they immediately see themselves as "kingdom laborers" who have a growing heart for other people to meet Jesus too!

Before we wrap up this session, let's touch base about our personal spiritual journey. If you are new to the group, or if you haven't taken the time to share, would you tell us about your journey of faith? Can you recall a time when you decided to invite Jesus to be your personal Savior and Lord? Please take this chance to share with us, or ask ANY questions you may have. Maybe you are not new to the group, but you have questions too. Now would be a perfect time to ask anything at all!

stop & talk... It's show and tell time! (but only if you really want to)

Now let's take a few moments to pray for God to reveal Himself to us all as we seek to understand who He is and what it would mean to surrender our lives to Him this week.

your coach will pray to end your time...

discover the life week #4:

Life is really all about practice

PRACTICE #1...Life-giving Prayer

Share with each other how your second week of practicing to become a "walking-worshipper" went. Did you remember to pray "life-giving prayers" as you were doing your normal everyday life? If you didn't, you can try again this week...or this next moment! If you did, could you sense an impact on your heart from it?

stop & talk... Tell the group what happened this week.

Let's add another dimension to our worship of God this week. We are going to consider who God is in comparison to the people and things we love. In Psalm 63:3, David says,

> "Because Your loving kindness is <u>better</u> than life,
> my lips will praise you!"

The truth is that God is better than everyone and everything else in life. As always, it is true whether it feels like it or not! It's important for us to get specific about what and how. We will do that by filling in the blank below in different ways.

"God you are better than _____ because _____."

Example: God you are better than <u>food</u>, because
<u>What you offer goes deeper.</u>
<u>What you offer is lasting.</u>
<u>What you offer doesn't go straight to my thighs.</u>
<u>What you offer doesn't raise my cholesterol.</u>
<u>What you offer doesn't leave me feeling empty.</u>

stop & talk & make a list...Let's do "things" first. But let's make them significant ones. The more important they are to you, the more powerful it will be to see that God is much better.

God you are better than _____

because _____.

God you are better than _____

because _____.

God you are better than _____

because _____.

Now let's consider how people have met needs in our lives that really only God can meet. Let's step out and declare that God is better than the people in our lives:

God you are better than people because _____

_____

_____

_____

_____

_____

stop & pray... Now, let's worship God together in Life-giving Prayer using the sentences we formed above...

stop & talk... Take a few minutes to talk about how you felt while we were "worshiping God without music." If you were quiet during prayer, please share why you didn't speak up. Remember we don't want anyone to feel pressure to do anything they aren't ready to do. You are in charge, and we hope you feel free to be real about how you feel!

Worship God all week by telling Him how much better He is than everyone and everything else you love! Discover how powerful it is when you pray out loud. When you are alone (and no one is looking!), give it a try.

PRACTICE #2...Life-giving Truth

Did you remember to connect the truth, "God is enough," with your disappointments and frustrations? If so did it make a difference?

stop & talk... Share with each other how the truth "God is enough," affected your heart and life this week.

We will continue to remind ourselves of our first three truths:

I am so loved.

God is here.

God is enough.

Remember, these are examples of truths you can discover in your own reading and study of the Bible as you ask yourself that important question, "What is God inviting me to believe?" Your truth might come from an author or speaker who is quoting the Bible or from your own Bible reading.

What is important is that it comes from the Bible and that you take it to heart. Getting it into our heads is much easier than getting it into our hearts! That's why we recommend that you focus on one truth for a whole week. We offer the six truths of this **dtl** group to teach you how to identify them for yourself for the rest of your life. Well, and because we feel that these six truths are foundational to a healthy relationship with God!

There is also an appendix in the back of this book that will help you with learning how to read and identify Life-giving Truth for yourself during your own reading of the Bible.

This week we will add another important truth to our understanding of God and ourselves in relationship with Him. Here's the truth...

"I'm enough for God."

This truth is a difficult one to grasp. We're going to take a little extra time to discuss this one because we believe it is the core of the gospel of grace and foundational to authentic and life-giving relationship with Him.

The idea that "I'm enough for God" goes against the grain of what some of us have picked up along the way. It's the opposite of the essence of most religious systems. It doesn't even feel right to say it out loud. How could I, in all of my weakness and failure, ever be enough for God? The answer is, of course, "I can't," if God actually *needs* something from me.

But here's the key:

*God's nature and character is dependent
on nothing outside of Himself.*

If God's self-esteem was in any way based on who I am and how I behave, and if He was hoping that I would come through in order to complete Him in some way, then He would always be disappointed in me. Of course it is ridiculous to think that God would have any such limitations.

Think about it. He is completely self-sufficient. He is the God of the Universe. He created it all, He sustains it all. He had no beginning, He has no end. He is not limited by space or time. Can any part of His well-being be dependent on our behavior? Of course not. He is God and, as He said in His Bible, "He knows that we are but dust."

The truth that "I'm enough for God" has NOTHING to do with *who I am* and everything to do with *who He is*! This is the gospel of grace. It is laid out best in the New Testament book of Romans.

Consider these thoughts drawn straight from the Bible:

1. *God would always be disappointed with me* IF...
He needed something from me.

But He doesn't. He is complete and perfect, lacking in nothing. The people in my life have needs and are disappointed when I don't meet them. God has no needs. Certainly none that I can meet, as it says in Acts 17:24, 25...

> *"The God who made the world and all things in it,*
> *since He is Lord of heaven and earth,*
> *does not dwell in temples made with hands;*
> *nor is He served by human hands,*
> ***as though He needed anything,***
> *since He Himself gives to all people*
> *life and breath and all things!"*

Wow! God is never disappointed because He has no needs.

stop & talk... Does that biblical concept make sense to you? Why/why not? Write down any thoughts here:

_____

_____

_____

_____

2. *God would always be disappointed with me* **IF...**
   He put any hope in me.

But God doesn't hope. Did you catch that? He never hopes. It is one of the ways He is very different from us. Read Romans 8:24...

> *For in hope we have been saved,*
> *but hope that is seen is not hope;*
> *for who hopes for what he already sees?*

As we know, God sees all things at all times! He knows every single choice that I will ever make, good or bad, for the rest of my life! He is already expecting everything I will do. One of the ways that God is completely different than us is that He sees all things and does not, therefore, hope. Here's the key:
If there is no hoping there can be no disappointing.
God is never disappointed with me because He does not hope.

stop & talk... Does that Biblical concept make sense to you? Why/ why not? Again, write down any thoughts here:

_____

_____

_____

_____

3. *God would always be disappointed with me* **IF...**
   my relationship with Him was based on my ability to live up to His standards.

It is not. He knew, and knows I cannot, and never will live to the standard of perfection required by His holiness.
So, from before the foundation of the universe, He planned to send His only Son, Jesus, to be executed as the substitute for me to satisfy the demands of true justice. Jesus paid the penalty in full for all

of my sins.

So now, **if I have given my life to Christ**, then God has made me <u>perfect</u> in His eyes by <u>dressing me</u> in the righteousness of Christ. By divine choice and divine sanction He traded Christ's righteousness for my unrighteousness. This absolute exchange is promised in many places in the Bible. Here are just a couple of them:

He made Him who knew no sin to BE SIN on my behalf that I might BECOME the righteousness of God in Him.

Galatians 3:27
*For all of you who were baptized into Christ
have clothed yourselves with Christ.*

Isaiah 61:10
*I will rejoice greatly in the Lord; my soul will exult in my God;
for He has clothed me with garments of salvation,
He has wrapped me with a robe of righteousness.*

Hebrews 10:14
*For by ONE offering, He has perfected for ALL TIME
those who are sanctified.*

That righteous perfection has absolutely NOTHING to do with what I *do* and EVERYTHING to do with what Jesus *did* for me when He died on the cross. We know that we could never be perfect before God based on our performance, no matter how good it sometimes is. Isaiah also said that even, "...*our righteousness is like filthy rags.*"

In the same way, I can't ever be bad enough to lose the perfection He has given me. Neither is based on my works. Both are based on His WORK (the cross and the resurrection). Both are based on His choice to give me this gift of grace. And make sure to notice, it is established "for all time!" God is never disappointed with me because I am in Christ and He sees only Christ's righteousness in me and on me. Amazing!

stop & talk... Does that biblical reality connect with your heart and mind? What questions do you have?

All that is left now is for me to stand firm in my belief in the truth that no matter how I am behaving, *I am enough for God!*

Are you ready to embrace the full implications of this incredible truth? Remember now, if something is ever true, then it is always true. That's the nature of truth. Here it is:

I am completely pleasing to Him even when I'm sinning.

Why? How? Because that sin was nailed to the cross upon which Jesus died. This sin I am right now committing was already transferred to Jesus when He traded His robe of righteousness.

He made Him who knew no sin to be sin on our behalf,
so that we might become the righteousness of God in Him.
2 Corinthians 5:21

God is not pleased with sinful behavior. Ever. He wants us to walk in His ways so that we will find the life He has offered us. God grieves over sin and it's harmful effects. But in order to experience how amazing grace really is, and the life it offers, we must embrace the reality that Jesus made us perfect in God's eyes, in the condition of the sins of the flesh. My good behavior can't make me more pleasing to Him and my sinful behavior can't make me less pleasing to Him. Saving faith transforms. That means that I am eternally and fully pleasing to Him, even in the moment of failure.

My sinful act isn't powerful enough to stain the righteousness of Christ that rests upon me by divine action! Neither is my sinful act strong enough to alter the attitude or opinion of Almighty God. That's where the freedom to live with Jesus and love Him comes from. All my guilt and shame are removed and I live under the smile of God all the time, no matter what!

That's grace. Now you know why we sing, "Amazing grace." More amazing than ever, right?

And by the way, these truths never make a *true believer want to take advantage of God's grace.* Some have worried that if we think God isn't disappointed with us even *while* we're sinning, we just might be tempted to go off sinning our brains out! That's one of the motivations our parents used with us, and we, perhaps have used with our children. But remember, God is very different from us.

The truth is, the more a true follower of Jesus Christ understands this gift of grace and the more fully he embraces it, the more his heart will be drawn to the one who provided it! We have nothing but desire to stay as close to Him as possible, living our lives in obedience and alignment with everything that He is. We have a growing appetite for holy living!

We don't live with an obligation to perform and a nagging

sense of shame. We have been freed from the paralyzing thought that we'll never be enough. We live in a permanent condition of freedom made possible by a bloodstained cross and an empty tomb. The freedom of grace is planted and rooted deeply in my totally surrendered heart. The result is that I love my Savior and desire uninterrupted relationship with Him!

But this truth is very hard to really embrace, because we make the mistake of viewing God like we view people. We feel the disappointment of people. It started early in our childhood. So we assume God must be like our parents, or other people. He must feel toward us like we feel toward others who disappoint us.

But He is not like us. He is above us. We are a ball of needs. He has no needs. We have learned the painful reality that when we behave well, people are pleased with us. Likewise, we have learned that when we behave poorly, people are disappointed with us. Much of our religious training taught us to think that the same is true with God! We have been conditioned to read the Bible that way. Our conclusions about God have been colored by this misunderstanding!

This powerful and exciting truth is grounded firmly in the Bible. If I don't believe it, I won't live in its power. I will experience the guilt and shame connected with my bad behavior, and my misunderstanding of God. I will be tempted to believe that Jesus is disappointed with me for my failures or impressed with my good choices.

If I don't live in this truth, I may be ***driven away from His love*** and into deeper faithlessness and sinful behavior due to the shame and guilt I experience. God's intention is that our sin would ***draw us to Him*** for grace and forgiveness! Romans 8:1 makes this clear...

> *"There is **NO condemnation**
> for those who are in Christ Jesus!"*

stop & talk... What is your response to these thoughts? Can you embrace this truth and begin to live in it this week or do you need more time to grasp it? Can you see the power this truth has to set you free from performance and the shame or pride that goes with it?

Tell yourself "I am enough for God" all week long. Make sure to do it in the midst of your failure, and watch for the impact it has on your heart!

PRACTICE #3...Life-giving Relationships

After that discussion, we're all more aware of something in us that needs God's touch. But first let's back up to this last week.

stop & talk... Share how healing prayer has impacted you over the last few weeks.

The freedom to embrace Life-giving Relationships and be real with each other comes from today's truth. God has and will delight in who I am regardless of all that is wrong with me. If I decide that His approval is all I need, I will be free to risk the rejection of man for the sake of growing as a person "in Christ." I will be free to stop pretending that I am perfect before people. My identity is defined by the fact that I am enough for God. So then, what does it matter what people think at any given moment?

stop & talk & pray... In light of our new understanding, does anyone want to share something for which they need healing prayer right now?

Before we move on, let's reemphasize that those who are totally surrendered to Jesus have been covered by grace. That grace is so great that it means God is pleased with you...PERIOD! He is never more or less pleased with you based on your behavior.

stop & pray... Real quick, your **dtl** coach is going to pray that this truth takes root in your heart during this coming week.

PRACTICE #4...Life-giving Impact

Did you remember to pray through your list daily? Did you remember to pray it when you found yourself in contact with people in general or specific ones on your list? Did you sense an impact on *your* heart? Can you see any signs that God is at work in people's hearts? Did you add anyone new to your list?

 **stop & talk...** Let's tell some Pray&Watch stories...

Remember that God's work is invisible and it often takes a while for us to see the evidence of it! Here are a few reasons we actively watch. Remember? It is "watching with anticipation."
1. We want to witness a miracle.

2. We'll be able to tell when a person is ready to listen to more of our story of being drawn to Jesus.

3. We'll discern the right time to share the really good news of God's love and grace and the hope we have in Jesus.

It would be easy if everyone was ready to hear. We could just run up and tell them. We could go door to door and tell everyone randomly. But we know that most people are not listening. We learn this through the "Parable of the Sower" recorded in Matthew 13...

> *Some seeds fell beside the road...*
> *others fell on the rocky places...*
> *others fell among the thorns...*
> *and others fell on the good soil and yielded a crop.*

We have the opportunity to sow seeds of truth into the lives of people. The problem is that we have no control over the condition of their hearts. If the soil of their hearts is not soft and ready, the seeds we sow will not take root.

So, we pray that the Holy Spirit will prepare their hearts to hear. We "Pray&Watch." We also realize that often times people's hearts are prepared through relationship. So we connect in whatever ways we can as we pray!

Before we pray is there anyone in the group who is new and hasn't told us your spiritual journey story? Is anyone processing your thoughts on faith in Jesus?

stop & talk... Please share with the group now. You might even want to ask the group members to put your name on their Pray&Watch list!

Remember, the most important decision of our lives is whether or not to invite Jesus Christ to be our personal Savior and Lord. That's why we have to keep talking about it. That's why we commit to praying for everyone we know, including everyone here in our group. Our hope is that each one is drawn to that place where they believe in Jesus and surrender their heart to Him!

stop & pray... Now Pray&Watch together...(your **dtl** coach will use this alternate version of the 5-second Prayer to start you off...)

"God only You can draw the heart of a person to Yourself.
Please, right now, wherever these people are,
send your Holy Spirit to speak to their hearts about their need for You.
Draw them to Yourself.
Raise them up to be Kingdom workers..."

Have a great week watching God at work in you and through you!

discover the life week #5:

Life is really all about practice

PRACTICE #1...Life-giving Prayer

Let's start by sharing our experience with "walking worship" during this last week.

stop & talk... How did you choose to worship God as a lifestyle this week?

Asking this question is a way for us to "take our spiritual temperature." Life-giving Prayer is really the best monitor of our growing intimacy with King Jesus and our growing passion for His kingdom. If we fail to monitor our connection with God, we will drift away from Him very quickly. The visible and tangible life we are living will overshadow our true purpose for living.

There is, perhaps, nothing as life-changing as a lifestyle of Life-giving Prayer! It is what King David is describing...

Psalm 37:4
*"Delight yourself in the Lord
and He will give you the desires of your heart."*

When we choose to let our hearts connect with who God is, we are delighted by Him. Ready to discover something profound?

God Himself IS the desire of our hearts!

He is planning to give you Himself! This will not happen simply because we say words of worship. It is essential that our hearts connect with the words we are saying to the point of being amazed! Then He becomes the desire of our heart. We no longer feel the need for what we formerly misunderstood and mis-defined as "the desires of our heart!"

Philippians 4:4 is an invitation to a lifestyle of worship:

"Rejoice in the Lord always, again I will say rejoice!"

When we think about who God is and what He has done for us, we can't help but rejoice! We rejoice when we finally realize we already have everything we need. No wonder Paul invites us to rejoice ALWAYS! If we have everything we need, why would we do anything other than rejoice…always?

- - - - - - - - - -

When we give God **glory** for who He is,
it *amazes* our hearts.

When we give God **honor** by choosing and submitting to Him,
it *purifies* our hearts.

When we give God **thanks** for all that He means to us,
it *thrills* our hearts!

When we **give God our needs**
it *brings peace* to our hearts.

- - - - - - - - - -

That is right where God wants us to live and the only place we can find real life. Our goal as we practice is to keep our hearts connected with His powerful and life giving presence as we live. This practice is the foundational one, and has everything to do with the effectiveness of the other three!

stop & pray... Spend some time in Life-giving Prayer together.

stop & talk... Spend a few moments debriefing about how we are doing and feeling about our group experience with Life-giving Prayer. Are you joining in? Why/Why not? What would need to change for your group to really get going in this shared experience? Any ideas?

Earlier we spoke about monitoring our intimacy with God. In reality, once a week in our **dtl group** is not nearly enough. Day by day and moment by moment God invites us to *"watch over our hearts"* if we want to find life (Proverbs 4:2).

As we make it a part of our Life-giving Lifestyle it will transform the group experience too. And remember, we're anticipating making Life Group a way of life after **dtl** is over. So we keep on practicing!

PRACTICE #2...Life-giving Truth

Spend some time sharing with each other how the truth, "I'm enough for God," affected your heart during this past week.

stop & talk... Process your thoughts and your questions with each other. This is a truth that requires lots of thought to grasp!

The fifth truth that we need to take to heart is found in Philippians 1:12-18. It is a truth that gives perspective and purpose to every circumstance in the everyday moments of our lives. We can choose to live for the mundane things of life or the people we love. We can choose to live for ourselves and sell out to our personal goals and dreams. We can live in an effort to please everyone around us. And of course there are a number of other purposes we could choose for our lives. The truth is, that few people even stop to consider what they *are* living for and whether or not it is a worthy purpose.

The truth these verses hold reveal another way to live. It is a truth that has everything to do with "finding what's worth living for!" Remember the human pursuit we talked about in week one? Everyone on the planet is trying to find what's worth living for whether they are conscious of it or not.

So let's read the following verses from Philippians 1 and see if we can answer the question that follows. By the way, the Apostle Paul wrote these words while he was in prison for no greater "crime" than talking to people about Jesus!

> *"Now I want you to know brethren that my circumstances have turned out for the greater progress of the gospel, so that my imprisonment in the cause of Christ has become well known throughout the whole Praetorian guard and to everyone else, and that most of the brethren, trusting in the Lord because of my imprisonment, have far more courage to speak the word of God without fear.*
>
> *Some to be sure, are preaching Christ even from envy and strife, but some also from good will. The latter do it out of love, knowing that I am appointed for the defense of the gospel; the former proclaim Christ out of selfish ambition rather than from pure motives, thinking to cause me distress in my imprisonment.*
>
> *What then?* **Only that in every way**, *whether in pretense or truth,* **Christ is proclaimed**; *and in this I will rejoice. Yes, I will rejoice!"*

stop & talk... What would you say is Paul's purpose for living?

One way to state the truth from Paul's words is this:

"What matters most, is people finding Jesus"

If we took a minute to compare life on this earth to eternity, we would quickly recognize that what happens here is not as important as what happens there. That is true simply because time has an end. We are on this earth only for a short time. It may seem long to us, but Psalm 90:10 puts that in perspective...

> *As for the days of our life, they contain seventy years or, if due to strength, eighty years, yet their pride is but labor and sorrow; for soon it is gone and we fly away.*

The Bible teaches that after time comes eternity. After life comes death, and then we stand before God for judgment. Only those who have put their trust in Jesus will be given eternal life. Hebrews 9:27, 28 says...

> *It is appointed for men to die once and after this comes judgment, so Christ also, having been offered once to bear the sins of many, will appear a second time for salvation without reference to sin to those who eagerly await Him.*

The verses are clear. I will die. I will face judgment. But Christ bore my sins on the cross so that I can have salvation. Am I one who eagerly awaits His coming at the end of time? If so, NO reference will be made to my sin when I stand before God!

On the other hand, for those who have not surrendered their lives to Him, Hell is a harsh reality. We don't like to think about it, so we rarely do. Some have just decided that if they close their eyes it isn't there. Some religions have written it out of their beliefs.

But the Bible is clear that many who live, work and play around us are going to spend eternity there unless they find Jesus. Perhaps some of us in this **dtl group** are still facing this reality.

As we have discussed in the context of "Pray&Watch," no human has the power to give faith or eternal life to another. It must come from the work of God's Spirit in their hearts drawing them to Himself. Jesus is speaking in John 6:44...

> *No one can come to Me*
> *unless the Father who sent Me draws him;*
> *and I will raise him up on the last day.*

Our most important job then is to "Pray" for the work of the Spirit to draw the hearts of people to Himself. Then, to fully engage with people, we "Watch," in an active way, because He is working! That's not so hard, except for the fact that we get so busy doing life that we forget what matters most: people finding Jesus!

Our Life-giving Truth for this week must be driven deeply into our hearts. That's why we must tell it to ourselves each day throughout the day. Here is a truth that needs to be plastered all over our homes and lives so that we are constantly reminded of it. Let's tell each other until this truth becomes the driving force of our earthly lives. Let's do it to the end that others find life in Him and we, and they find "what's worth living for!"

What matters most, is people finding Jesus!

PRACTICE #3...Life-giving Relationships

Are you embracing the concept of being "real" rather than pretending? Are you ready to take the risk of being real for the hope of being healed?

stop & talk... Share with each other any work you see God doing in your heart as a result of healing prayer.

Now go ahead and take the risk! Who senses something in their heart that is inconsistent with their faith, or simply feels "broken" or unmanageable?

stop & talk & pray... Who would like healing prayer?

PRACTICE #4...Life-giving Impact

Is "Pray&Watch" becoming part of our daily life? Are our lists growing? Is it affecting us? Can you see any signs, as you watch, that someone might be ready to "hear" the truth about Jesus and eternal life?

stop & talk... Let's share any stories we have related to "Pray&Watch."

stop & talk... Is anyone facing life's greatest "fork in the road?" Do you sense it is time to surrender fully to Jesus? It is our privilege to process with you so please don't hesitate to share your thoughts or feelings if you want to!

So, remember two things as you Pray&Watch this week:

1) If we try to tell someone about Jesus without respecting them, they won't listen to us!

2) If we try to tell someone about Jesus before God has worked in their hearts they won't believe us!

stop & pray... Now, do the most significant thing possible for a human being to do for another human being... Pray&Watch for real people to be drawn to Christ and become laborers for the Kingdom of God!

discover the life week #6:

Life is really all about practice

PRACTICE #1...Life-giving Prayer

stop & talk... Share one time you connected with God in worship this week.

stop & talk... Share one thing about God that amazes you and why.

     The most important part of Life-giving Prayer is that it causes our hearts to be aware of how amazing God is. It's easy to say things like "God knows everything," but until we ***stop*** and ***consider*** all that He knows, <u>very specifically</u>, it won't really amaze our hearts.
     It's when we compare what *He* knows with what *we* know that we are blown away by how different He is. We struggle to get our minds around who He really is. That's good! True worship has to leave us ***wondering***.
     Our God is so far beyond us that He will always be a mystery to us! We'll never fully comprehend who He is, nor will we understand why He does what He does. That is why our relationship with Him is based on faith and surrender. Take some time to think, to

contemplate and to wonder about the attributes we accept as part of God's nature. If we will, then we are able to get in touch with how worthy He is of our worship!

Before we pray together, let's just remember that praying in a group is different than praying alone. We have to learn how to do it.

As we pray today we're going to work at seeing it as a conversation. Try to listen to each other's prayers and let your heart respond by saying, "Wow!" Let's practice letting our hearts wonder about the words others are saying and what those words really mean so we can help each other get more in touch with who God really is.

To do this, we're going to limit our praises to only one attribute of God and then stick to it. Let's use God's omniscience, which means that God knows all things, as an example.

Here's how it might go:

Someone starts by saying,

"God I praise you because you know everything."

We could stop there, because it pretty much sums up the reality of His omniscience. But what if we kept going and someone else prayed saying,

"You know what I am thinking before I even think it!"

Now, if I was listening and pondering that statement, I might be moved to awe, and then be prompted to say,

"You know every motive, attitude and thought I keep hidden from everyone else!"

Now stay with it! That's an obvious invitation to everyone in the group to get personal about what God knows about their hearts! So our prayer time might continue with phrases like the following:

"You know my angry thoughts and love me anyway."

"You know my lustful heart, and forgive me."

"You know I am consumed with worry, and offer me rest."

It leads right into giving God honor…surrendering those parts of us He knows about…

"I surrender my anger, lust, and worry."

"I choose Your work in me over relief from the conditions that make me so mad."

"I choose Your will in that situation, and choose to rest."

Then we're right into giving God thanks…

> *"Thank you that these feelings don't have to rule me."*

> *"I am grateful that my lustful flesh is not who I am. Your power is greater. And Your love is better!"*

Of course, then we're ready to go right into life-giving requests, giving God our needs in the light of God's will and not ours!

> *"You know the past, the present, and every detail of the future, so take my anger and work in my heart to love that person I am angry at!"*

> *"I ask You to place deep love and respect in my heart for You, my wife, and for purity, that I might be Your man and do Your will"*

> *"Please work in Your perfect timing in my son's life as he makes decisions that seem to be dangerous and destructive to him and others around him. I release my worry to You."*

It's a powerful way to pray together, or alone! But it takes some getting used to. We're having a conversation together with God that is all about God. We must learn to listen to each other, give our hearts time to consider what someone else says. It's less about closed eyes and folded hands, or thinking about what you want to say next.

It's more about genuine conversation with God. He is actually present here as we pray! No, seriously, He is here. He is listening. And we are listening to God and to the others in our group, being stimulated to wonder *beyond* what they have said, and even add to what they said.

Let's try it together. First we'll have a time of giving praise to God. Then we'll choose Him, surrender to Him, thank Him and invite Him to work out His will through the things that are concerning us! Let's use God's omnipotence, that He is all-powerful.

Your **dtl** coach will start the group off with: *"God, it is amazing that You are the most powerful force in the universe."* As you pray, think about all the powerful forces of nature. He spoke them into place! Their power came out of His person! Think about sin's power that seems so intense over our lives. He rules over it and gets His way through it. Think about powerful emotions, powerful people, and powerful positions.

After you surrender to His power, you can give thanks for the wisdom, love, grace, and compassion that dictate how He uses His power in our lives. You can then ask for the unleashing of His power into your life and circumstances!

stop & pray... *"God, it is amazing that You are the most powerful force in the universe."*

Before you move on to the next practice, pick another attribute of God that you can all "wonder" in prayer about throughout this week. You can talk next week about the significant moments it created. We recommend thinking about God's sovereignty. It means that He is in control of EVERYTHING! Get ready to struggle through whether or not you really believe it!

PRACTICE #2...Life-giving Truth

stop & talk... Share how last week's truth impacted your heart during the week: *"What matters most is people finding Jesus."*

Now for this week's truth:

"It works if I work it into my heart!"

Let's read Deuteronomy 6:4-9 to see the Biblical explanation of this truth...

(4)" Hear O Israel! The Lord is our God, the Lord is one! (5)You shall love the Lord your God, with all your heart and with all your soul and with all your might. (6) These words, which I am commanding you today, shall be on your heart. (7) You shall teach them diligently to your sons, and shall talk of them when you sit in your house and when you walk by the way and when you lie down and when you rise up! (8) You shall bind them as a sign on your hand and they shall be as frontals on your forehead. (9) You shall write them on the door posts of your house and on your gates."

stop & talk... Let's talk about how this passage describes a "lifestyle of faith."

1. How is true devotion described in verse 5?

2. Where does verse 6 tell us to put God's Word?

3. What does verse 7 invite us to do with God's word as we live out in our everyday lives?

4. What do you think verses 8 & 9 are all about? How does this reveal the depth of our devotion to God as a way of life?

5. Do these verses describe your lifestyle? How? Why? Why not?

Who do you talk to about God in your everyday life?
Your kids? Your husband? Your self? God? Friends?

Put their name(s) here:_____

Consider how much it stimulates your spiritual growth just to come to **dtl** once a week and talk about God with each other. How much more would it impact you if you spoke daily with the people with whom you live, work, and play? What if you made a pact with your family members/roommates/co-workers etc. to help each other keep the truth of the week in front of you?

Here's a couple of ideas:

- Tell your family what the truth is and talk about what it means.
- Challenge each other to talk about it all week long.
- Ask your children to remind you of the truth daily.
- Remind each other every morning.
- Ask each other every night.
- Share stories with each other about how it impacted your day.

- Call on the phone and ask if they can quote the truth of the week.
- Encourage each other to try again tomorrow.
- Send a text message to someone with the truth!

stop & talk... Which of these ideas do you see working in your home or with a friend?

stop & talk... When it comes to Life-giving Truth, the whole point is that it gets to our hearts. Which of these statements do you think is <u>more</u> true?

1. If it's on your heart you will talk about it a lot.
2. If you talk about it a lot, it will be on your heart.

Talk about the slight difference between those two statements...

Sometimes we don't talk about things on our heart because we don't think it is appropriate. Maybe we think people don't want to hear about it. On the other hand, it's pretty hard for us to talk about something over and over without having that thing take deep root in our heart! The more we hear ourselves talking about God the more real He will be to us. Maybe we can't always be talking to other people about God, but we CAN always be talking to *ourselves* about Him. We can always be talking to *Him* about Him!

Thinking about God and His truth doesn't come naturally to us in the context of everyday living.
We have to re-train our minds to do it.
A lifestyle of faith is ours if we work the 4 Life-giving Practices, but IT ONLY WORKS IF YOU WORK IT! We can see every situation and relationship in all of life as an opportunity to work the practices, or we can let life "work" us! It's our choice.

stop & talk... Are you working your lifestyle of faith, or is your lifestyle "working" you?

PRACTICE #3...Life-giving Relationships

stop & talk... Share with each other how God seems to be working through your healing prayers for each other.

Is there anyone who has something going on in their hearts that they would like God to heal?

stop & talk & pray... Would you like to ask for prayer? Would it be ok for us to gather around you and lay our hands on you as we pray?

PRACTICE #4...Life-giving Impact

stop & talk... In general, then, how is your Pray&Watch lifestyle coming along? Is Pray&Watch becoming a lifestyle? How is it changing the way you see people? How is it affecting your kids or your friends? Are you seeing any impact in the lives of people?

You know, we are praying and watching because we believe the greatest gift and the most important decision that any human being can make is to give their life to Jesus Christ and be certain that they will go to heaven when they die. Is there anyone in the group who would like to talk about that?

We've spent these six weeks together in **dtl**, and if you have not surrendered your life to Christ yet, share with the group what you are thinking and feeling.

stop & talk... We are all on a journey. Anyone on that part of the journey marked by surrendering for the first time?

stop & pray... OK, now let's Pray&Watch together!

Holy Spirit, please draw the hearts of these people to Yourself and make them kingdom laborers!

Let's wrap up our **dtl** group...

If your group has been a mix of men and women, find another room and have the guys go there. Let's take a couple minutes to discuss the idea of making Life Group a way of life all your life. We have come to see that life is all about practice. These 4 Life-giving Practices have added a new dimension to our spiritual journey and we want to keep going.

We've discovered that it works best, if we want to "go to the next level" to have what we call "gender-based" groups. You know, sometimes guys won't open up about some things if there are women present, and vice-versa.

So here comes another "fork in the road." You ready to take the next step?

stop, move to another room, and talk...

Now that you are in two groups (male and female), answer the following questions, and discuss possible meeting times for the formation of two new Life Groups, one for the guys, and one for the ladies.

1. Now that you have spent six weeks learning the Life-giving Practices how do you feel about making Life Group a way of life?

2. Could this group of men or women become your regular Life Group?

3. Who do you know that would like Life Group?

4. Are there some other people you would like to invite for a **dtl group** for six weeks?

5. Would you feel equipped to "coach" a new **dtl group** using this book?

Welcome to the adventure of
the Life-giving lifestyle!

read on your own... Sometime this week, read the next two pages...

appendix #1:
A Life-giver's Covenant

We are Life-givers.

We are *"finding what's worth living for."* We have come to believe that it both begins and ends in an intimate relationship with Jesus. We are bringing our faith together with our lives, creating a lifestyle of faith. We choose **Life Group** as a way of life for the rest of our lives, *knowing that we cannot do it alone.* We work 4 Life-giving Practices, *knowing that no one else can do it for us.*

Many of us have tried doing all the right things. While "religion" provided structure for our lives and the encouragement to press on, our hearts hungered for more. We want to *experience* the satisfaction only Jesus can give.

We believe that "what's worth living for" can only be found in a *growing intimacy with the King,* and a *growing passion for His Kingdom.* We want to become Life-givers so we are purposeful about making 4 Life-giving Practices our lifestyle. It only works if we work it into our hearts.

Life-giving Prayer is more about being *with* God than getting something *from* God. As we continuously praise Him, choose Him, surrender to Him, celebrate what He means to us, and focus on HIS will, we are becoming "walking worshippers."

Life-giving Truth is a focus on the *truth* in God's word. We find that truth by asking, "what does God want me to believe?" Then we head into life choosing to ponder, celebrate, and connect ourselves with it's powerful reality, letting it change us from the inside out. (*The truth shall set you free - John 8:32*).

Life-giving Relationships happen when we finally grow weary of pretending. We find freedom, respect, and acceptance in being real. We hope in the promise of James 5:16, *"Confess your sins to one another and pray for each other so that you may be healed."*

Life-giving Impact is a "Pray&Watch" lifestyle. We pray: *"Holy Spirit, draw the heart of this person to Yourself and make him a kingdom laborer,"* as we live, work and play among real people in our everyday lives, actively watching God work!

We work at living the practices all week long. At Life Group we tell stories about their impact on us and then experience them together. There is no end date, but we are all free to invite new people, attend more than one group, switch to another group, quit attending, or start a new group at any time. Who do you know that needs a Life Group?

Spiritual life is an *opportunity* not a *duty*. We focus on the grace that invites us to try again, instead of self-condemning. We seek to be honest, instead of pretending. We share only about our own issues and not the wrongs of others. We pray for each other, rather than giving advice. We don't expect our humanness to be *cured*. We're learning to walk with God in the midst of it! And we believe that God gives us our next breath to praise Him and for the sake of those that are perishing without Him.

Life-givers have seven core values that guide us.

1. **Surrender:** choosing and yielding to God. When I surrender, God is seen.

2. **Dependency:** we are desperate for God to work, so we pray. Prayer IS the work!

3. **Immersion:** because people find Jesus through relationships. We're here for the sake of the lost, so we immerse our lives among them.

4. **Authenticity:** choosing to believe that real is better than perfect.

5. **Graciousness:** people often say, "You must live up to my standards or go." God says, "You can't possibly live up to my standards, so COME!" We need grace, so we give grace.

6. **Focus:** because people are eternal. What matters most is people finding Jesus.

7. **Multiplication:** we're asking God to use us to reach two who will each reach two more, who will then reach two more, every year for the rest of our lives. We are becoming life-giving multipliers!

It's a fork in the road. Will you take it?

Will you live it?

sign: _____ date: _____

appendix #2:

How do I do Life-giving Truth without **dtl**?

The goal of **dtl** was to give us an experience of the 4 Life-giving Practices so that our appetite would settle for nothing less from now on! We hope they could become your lifestyle. Most of us need to stay connected to at least one other person in order to make it stick. If you agree on using this structure, it will work well in any small group. Just move from practice to practice, telling stories and then practicing each one together.

Since all of the practices are based on the Life-giving Truths of the Bible, this is the one of the four that needs more attention. Our offerings of Life-giving Truth throughout the weekly sessions provided you with an experience of Life-giving Truth. From now on, you need to be equipped with the ability to discover it for yourself.

It comes from an "outside source" (your personal reading, a sermon, or a Bible study you might be involved in). In any case, it must come from God's word. We have found that if the Bible is to come alive to us, we have to ask questions of it as we read. The key to finding the Life-giving Truth in a passage is to ask this question: "What is this passage inviting me to believe?" or, "What would I have to believe to be a person who lives out this passage?" For most of us, this is an additional question than those we've been taught to ask in the past.

For those who have a church home, we suggest you use a truth drawn from your pastor's sermon each week. You can also draw it from a book of the Bible you are reading through, or another book or study written around God's Word. The key will be your commitment to identifying a truth you will believe, tell yourself, and practice "living with," being diligent to tell stories about it the next time you meet with your group.

In order to be ready to live in a truth it's important to focus the time you spend together on that one truth rather than trying to discuss the whole passage or chapter you read. You want to go home understanding it's implications and with a vision for how it will impact your heart. That is essential if you want to experience the life connected with the truth!

Here's an example using Matthew 6:25-34.
The instruction is *"Do not worry!"*
To go into a week determined not to worry results in discouragement and frustration…and most of the time more worry! But a closer look reveals several Life-giving Truths. If we choose to

practice believing even one of them, it will begin to impact our hearts. We will have entered into a process leading us into a heart set free from anxiety. Worry is a heart issue, that actually grows out of the beliefs that are firmly rooted in our hearts! All the changed behavior in the world could never be as powerful as a changed heart!

If you were to take some time to look more closely at this paragraph of Scripture, you would see for yourself all these truth statements buried there:

Verse 25 - *"Life is about more than this."*
Verse 27 - *"Worry can't change a thing!"*
Verses 28-32 - *"God knows about my needs."*
"God cares about my needs."
"God is meeting my needs perfectly."
"I can trust God to take care of me."
"God has the ability to meet my needs"
"Whatever I have is enough"
Verse 33 - *"What matters today is God's kingdom."*

Now select the one that most speaks to your heart's need for transformation. Imagine how it could change your life if your heart learned to believe it and live as if it were true all the time!

We've discovered that one week of telling yourself a Life-giving Truth is enough to make it come alive and keep it in your heart, ready to be drawn on in every day's realities. One week of daily review will ensure that it sticks with you for genuine life change. More Scriptural truth than that is often too much to process.

You'll be amazed, after only a few weeks, how powerful the truth has become in your life. Fill your home and family with it as well, and everyone will live in truth!

We've provided you with another, more thorough "training tool" in appendix #4 for more examples and some work at learning how to identify Life-giving Truth on your own using a good variety of biblical passages.

If you want the thrill of discovering God's heart; if you want to grow in your ability to feed yourself on the truth of God's word; if you are serious about becoming a Life-giver, it's a "must read!" If you want to enter into the next phase of your impact as a kingdom laborer, and coach a dtl, or be better equipped at implementing the 4 Life-giving Practices in the context of a Life Group, or any small group for that matter, then take advantage of this training!

appendix #3:

50, or so, "tips" for making dtl groups more effective...

In General...

1. Anytime you feel stuck on something, come back to read these "tips" again.
2. Always emphasize the idea of moment by moment practicing of the 4 Life-giving Practices over attendance at stuff, knowing stuff, or whatever other stuff.
3. Practice is the opposite of performance. We are practicing, not performing.
4. The most important thing is that we are each one deepening in our heart connection with God.
5. The big picture thing is that we are cultivating a lifestyle that actually offers and brings life to the people around us.
6. We're real...we're in process...God will do it in His time.
7. The very best group coach is the one who is living the 4 Life-giving Practices every day.
8. Get familiar with the material before you start your group.
9. Make sure you've gotten answers to your own questions before you start a session.
10. Avoid "ad-libbing." Just read through it. Chances are, the thoughts you add are coming right up.
11. The best groups are the ones that have a variety of people, coming form a variety of places. Celebrate that!
12. Always allow/encourage people to be themselves.
13. Resist the temptation to skip over the questions about how the week went on each of the four practices. This is how we "take our temperature" and make the practices take root in our everyday lives.
14. Always have a story to tell on all four practices. The "smaller" the story the better! Show people that the littlest thing is a great story. Here are a few examples:
    Life-giving Prayer –
    "I saw the sky and it reminded me of how big God is!"

> Life-giving Truth –
> "*I was doing the dishes and thought – God is here.*"
> Life-giving Relationships –
> "*When my anger rose up, I remembered you guys praying for me.*"
> Life-giving Impact –
> "*Yesterday I ran into Joe and we talked about the weather. As he walked away I prayed for him again to know Jesus.*"

15. And coach, if you don't have a story, be honest! You are practicing too!

In Life-giving Prayer...

16. Address the idea that there is no wrong way to pray.
17. Point out that it is worth the work to learn to be God-centered instead of self-centered, and that takes training.
18. Invite the group to love interruptions…especially during the prayer times! Let's be real!
19. Don't be afraid to do a little gentle coaching of prayer times.
20. Take care not to discourage those stepping out into the frightening waters of "public praying" with too much correction.
21. When someone shares a story or prays a prayer that is not worshipful, affirm that any kind of prayer is GOOD, but that our goal is to make it about God rather than us. Brainstorm together on how that story could have been shared with just the "God part" or how that request could have stimulated worship. For example:
    > If someone prays for the safety of another, it could lead to worshipping God that He knew before that person was born whether or not they would be injured. Not only that but He is in control of it and using it for good. God is purposeful in a wise and loving way. But He cares more about our hearts than the safety of our bodies! It's also really cool to remind ourselves that God will be enough for them and us even if they do get injured!
22. Don't hesitate to get alone with a particularly counter-productive pray-er and ask for their assistance in focusing the group on this new manner of praying.
23. If someone is uncomfortable praying out loud at group challenge them to three things: 1) Ask God to overcome the fear (use healing prayer time for that!) 2) Return to the list in week one, having the whole group use it, so the words are there for you and get comfortable speaking out during prayer time, and 3) practice talking out loud to God when you are

alone or with small children. It's a good way to get comfortable hearing your own voice talking out loud to God!

In Life-giving Truth...
24. Remind people that we are not doing Bible study in the same way they may have approached it before. We are seeking to make the truths revealed in the Bible verses real in our hearts and everyday lives. Belief is our goal, not knowledge, and not even obedience. We believe that knowledge without belief is arrogance and that God-honoring obedience flows out of absolute, heart-level belief.
25. Invite people to consider the truths that we discuss. Arguing is not necessary. Neither is convincing. Another person's process may require more time than you have right now and that's cool.
26. Don't feel like you have to have answers to all the questions that people might ask. It's ok to not know!
27. Don't be threatened if people disagree.
28. Thank people for expressing opinions and disagreement.
29. Present the truth statements with confidence. They may feel new to some in your group. Don't let it surprise you.

In Life-giving Relationships...
30. Be the first to ask for prayer. This models openness and vulnerability.
31. Be bold about encouraging the laying on of hands. Acknowledge that it feels a bit weird. Also celebrate how cool it is to be so purposefully supportive of each other.
32. There is no sin or brokenness that is too crazy to be addressed in **dtl**. Real is better than perfect.
33. Be ready to do some serious coaching after people share their problems for too long, or with too much detail.
34. Be ready to respectfully say, "Let's remember that we don't name the names of wrong-doers, or even focus on their wrongs, but on our own brokenness."
35. Be ready to do some serious coaching when people start giving advice or minimizing the problem. Often people will do that in their prayers. It feels like a good time to preach a sermon! Jump right in after someone shares and suggest that we pray. If you don't jump in, the group loses focus on the power and purpose of healing prayer.
36. Be sure there's at least one prayer for Jesus to heal this person's heart, specifically for their sin/brokenness issue. People will, as they are learning this kind of focused prayer, to

pray all around it for "strength" and stuff. Everything except supernatural healing by the authority and touch of Jesus Christ!
37. It's ok if nobody has anything to share, but be sure to ask if anyone needs prayer every time. Sometimes our sense of awkwardness for these "private" things welcomes negligence.

In Life-giving Impact...
38. Remember, everyone's at a different point on their journey and that is good. It's a privilege to join someone on their journey and walk alongside.
39. Always conclude your Pray&Watch time by praying for anyone who is in the group who has yet to receive Christ as Savior. Do it openly and lovingly and respectfully. It is the coolest thing to openly accept and honor people whose lives are being altered right before our eyes!
40. Don't ever hesitate or apologize for presenting the truth of Jesus Christ as our risen Savior and Lord, and that faith and surrender to Him is the only way to salvation.
41. Be open about the fact that you've put all the group members on your Pray&Watch list and that you hope they have put you on theirs.
42. Mention that a group member might even want to put their own name on their own Pray&Watch list.
43. Never hesitate to encourage someone to meet Jesus while on the journey.
44. Remember that it is not people genuinely searching for Jesus who are nervous about being open in the journey process, it is usually people with lots of church background who get cautious.
45. We are not doing espionage work here. There are no secret strategies, but open hearts and conversations.
46. When someone new comes, and you explain the heart of Pray&Watch, let them know that they have been prayed for and encourage them by helping them see that their presence at group is not an accident, but evidence that God is working in their heart.

In the case of quiet people...
47. Let everyone know that quietness is ok here. The world is uncomfortable with quiet, but at **dtl** quiet is ok.
48. Make sure to ask quiet people how they are feeling. Assure them that it is perfectly fine to be quiet, but that we all want to hear their hearts when they are ready.
49. Make it a point to ask people who are silent to join in from

time to time. Make it easy for them to decline, but don't hesitate to make the invitation.
50. Sometimes you might want to go around the circle for sharing on a given question so as to prompt larger participation. Just make sure they know they can "pass"
51. Sometimes silence lends itself to "filler" by the too-talkative." Always be ready to jump in and get the group back on task.
52. Sometimes people are quiet because another said what they wanted to say. Invite people to repeat another person's prayer, even if it's word for word, if it expresses their own heart!

In spiritual journey story-telling...
53. Celebrate every person for their openness to share even though their story might be a bit crazy.
54. In week #1, when you share spiritual journey stories, go first, be _very brief_, and be clear on the when and how you gave your life to Christ. Set the stage.
55. Encourage everyone that the only right story is the true story! Let's start off the first week by being real. This sets the stage for future realness!
56. Never be shocked. Create an environment that makes people feel like they are going to find acceptance among us no matter what.
57. Sometimes longer-term Christians struggle to embrace the presence of seekers or skeptics. Be prepared to show everyone how cool it is that we can talk out loud about our beliefs before, during and after a person accepts Jesus as Savior, and the Bible as the true word of God, and that we respect and love each other even if someone never chooses to believe as we believe. This is still a great place to be friends!

appendix #4:

Discovering Life-giving Truth...
...on your own
...as a way of life.

A word to church leaders, teachers, preachers...
in fact anyone interested in becoming more proficient
at gleaning Life-giving Truth to believe from the Bible...

When it comes to continuing to practice the 4 Life-giving Practices as a way of life for the rest of your life, "LG Truth" is the tough one. Not because the process is difficult (we're going to share *how* with you below), but because it is counter to our current cultural approach to the Scriptures. For these reasons:

1. We've been told we need a teacher/preacher to feed us, so we are not as prone to feed ourselves (a goal of all people growing to maturity).
2. We tend to return to treating the Bible like facts we are supposed to be informed about or behaviors we are supposed to conform to.
3. We have to be intentional about searching for the truth to believe that is imbedded in any and every passage we might read; in any and every sermon God might bring to our ears; any and every "Bible Study" we might participate in.

Proverbs 2
My son, if you will receive my words
and treasure my commandments within you...
incline your heart to understanding...
if you seek her as silver and search for her as for hidden treasures;
then you will discern the fear of the Lord
and discover the knowledge of God...
For wisdom will enter your heart...
discretion will guard you, understanding will watch over you.

If we're not intentional then we will slip backward. So we have put the following material together to provide a little extra dose of "how to" on the second of the 4 Life-giving Practices. We hope it will equip you to integrate God's word at a heart level as a way of life, all your life, teaching others to do the same.

Remember, it is not our goal to conquer the Bible, but to be conquered by it (Hebrews 4:12, 13). It is not enough to know the word of God, but to have our hunger satisfied by intimate knowledge of the God of the word!

Some more typical approaches to God's word:
We typically open the Bible looking for information to know, instructions to obey, and principles to apply. While these are all good, they leave out the singularly unique power of the word of God. It is the revelation of a person, and the revelation of absolute truth from the heart of the One who created all of life. These things were written that we might believe (John 20:31)!

An even better approach to God's Word:
Hidden in these writings is a person (John 1:1). He alone holds the words of eternal life. I go looking for Him. I go asking Him to reveal Himself to me. I see every word as a means to understanding who He is and connecting myself to what He says. I ask myself the question,
"*Why did God include these words here?*"
"*What does this tell me about God?*"
"*What does He want me to believe about Him, about life, about people, about myself?*"
Even when the passage is instructional, we ask,
"*What would I need to believe that would prompt me to naturally live out these instructions?*"

We must choose, as Proverbs 2 calls us, to search for those truths, and "know" those truths as John 8:32 calls us. This "knowing" is of the biblical variety. That is, an intermingling of my heart with the living word of God that results in the two becoming one.

The process of Life-giving Truth:
- Open to the beginning of a book of the Bible.
- Pray for God to give you understanding.
- Read a portion of it. Look for facts, instructions and principles.
- Then ask God, "*What are you calling me to believe?*"
- Answer that question in as many words as necessary to define it well.
- Now summarize this "truth to believe" in as many short and simple statements as you can. There will be more than one.
- Pick the one that seems to make the deepest connection with your heart.
- Take it with you all week long, saying it over and over again.
- Choose to believe it whether it feels true or not. ***If it is ever true, it is always true!***

Specific examples for how to find and use Life-giving Truth:

How to use this instructional section:

We've offered some sample discoveries below. Look up the verses listed after each number. Go through the process above. Read the verses. Pray for understanding. Look for facts, instructions, and principles. Then ask God to show you what it is that He is calling you to believe in this passage. What would you need to believe in order to obey it from the heart? Summarize the truth in as many short and simple statements as you can.

After taking those steps, read what has been written for you in each of the samples. Compare what *you* saw with the examples we provide. Then finish the process as listed above. Do these examples one at a time, trying it first on your own and then comparing your thoughts to the example we've provided. Do only one or two at a sitting, for practice. Part of the practice is to take your discovered truth through your entire week. That's when it takes root, changes our beliefs, and transforms us from the inside out. So we suggest that you use this practice tool the same way you'll approach the Bible's truths later in dtl or in your on-going life beyond dtl! By the way, you will find yourself getting better with each try!

1. Psalm 24:1 (Drawing truths from the poetical writings of the Bible)
"The World is the Lords and all it contains.
The earth and those who dwell in it."

This verse does not contain instructions to obey. There is information to know, and truth to believe. We could summarize this verse with either of these statements: *"Everything belongs to God"* or *"God owns everything and everyone!"*

There is a Life-giving Truth statement for you to take into your week. However, if you were to take a few more minutes and contemplate what that actually means you might come up with statements that will connect it a little more powerfully to your heart. Such as ...
"Nothing is mine."
"I am not mine."
"You are not mine."
"That is not mine."
Another way to say it is...
"That's God's."
"You're God's."
"I'm God's."
"Everything is God's."

If you also spend some time thinking about what it means to possess something you would come up with truth statements

connected to the control and freedom He has as the owner of all things...
"That's God's, He can do whatever He wants to with it!"
"I'm God's, He can do whatever He wants to with me."
"You are God's, He can do whatever He wants to with you."
"You are my child, but I don't own you and I can't control you."
"Since nothing is mine, I have ultimate control over nothing."

You might also contemplate the responsibility that comes with ownership...
"It's not ultimately up to me, I'm not the owner!"

Once you've contemplated all of the things that God is calling you to believe through these words of the Bible, you can pick one statement to take with you. The cool thing is that it will be flooded with all kinds of meaning because of all of these thoughts that you considered!

Now imagine that you have worked to retrain your heart to believe that nothing belongs to you. You have made statements all week long about the fact that your *things* are not yours. At the end of the week, your house burns down. What do you think will be your first response? Can you see how your heart would be equipped to deal with that tragedy in a different way than before you practiced Life-giving Truth?

Let's look at one more example from poetical writings. The book of Proverbs is such a favorite and many read from it daily. It is also very behaviorally driven, resulting in much of the "try-harder" brand of Christianity many have settled for in the church today! Let's give it a go...

Proverbs 13:1 (Drawing truths from the poetical writings of the Bible)
"A wise son accepts his father's discipline,
but a scoffer doesn't listen to rebuke."

Here's how we've classically treated a verse like this:
"It's a sin to scoff."
"We should respect and obey our parents."
"I should be wise."
"I should stop rebelling against my father."
"I should listen to rebuke."

Instead, consider these Life-giving Truths:
"The path to wisdom requires humility."
"I need other people's input in my life."
"Confrontation is part of love.'

"It's good for me to listen when I don't want to."
"I can learn from others."
"I need to be teachable."
"I can learn from you."
"I need humility."
"It's good for me to be corrected."
> (Note our examples of different ways of saying the same thing. We include this so as to put to rest any thought or worry about finding exactly the right words.)

"I don't have to be afraid of criticism."
"Humility can embrace humiliation."
"I hurt myself when I resist instruction."

Do you hear the difference between instructions to obey and beliefs to make your own? Obedience, by itself, lasts a moment, but beliefs reshape an entire life. Again, that all important question:

***How does God want to shape my beliefs
with the words of this passage?***

2. Ephesians 4:29 (Drawing truths from the didactive writings of the Bible)
> "Let no unwholesome word proceed from your mouth,
> but only such a word as is good for edification
> according to the need of the moment
> that it may give grace to those who hear."

The instruction is very clear: Don't let a word come out of your mouth unless it will give grace! There is no truth stated in those words so we must ask ourselves: *"What do we need to believe in order to live out these instructions?"*

First let's imagine ourselves with a simple focus on the instructions. We will go into our day, determined to keep anything bad from coming out of our mouths (no cussing, sarcasm, criticism, etc.). How effective do you think that would be? Imagine a day where we actually controlled our tongues. Have we changed from the inside out, or just succeeded in managing our behavior…for a time?

Instructions create a "gotta try harder" mentality. That mentality will naturally lead to one of two things: 1) Failure (guilt, shame, discouragement), or 2) Success (often resulting in pride, self-righteousness), rather than a desperate appreciation for God Himself and His grace!

Now let's consider some truths God is inviting us to believe:
"My words have power."
"I get to choose how I use my words."
"I can be a grace giver."
"People need grace."

If I go through a week reminding myself over and over again that *"my words have power"* I will be aware and motivated to use them for good in the lives of the people I love (or even hate!). I'll be more aware of the potential I have to hurt or build up another. I will be more likely to notice their impact, good or bad, and to experience how it feels to hurt another or build them up. When I fail, I will be powerfully reminded of the truth. I will also become more aware of how much I need God's grace flowing through me and His healing power in my own heart!

If I go through a week telling myself the truth *"people need grace,"* then I will be more likely to use my words for building up even people who frustrate me...even people who I hate!

I will be training myself to look past the surface of the people in my life, remembering that everyone has stuff going on that makes them in need of grace. I will see people more, judging their behavior less. It doesn't usually look like it on the outside, but there is so much going on in all of us. My awareness, because I'm telling myself the truth, makes me much more likely to choose to be gracious. Why? My perspective on people has actually been changed. I'm less focused on me and more focused on others.

How much better than wasting this passage on setting a goal to not cuss for the 167th time? Let's stop robbing the Bible of its Life-giving power! We are discovering the life! We are discovering the true and deep power of Life-giving Truth!

Can you see the way these truths have the power to change who we are from the inside out? Of course the source of their power is not the *words* themselves it is the God behind the words. That's why it is okay to put them into your own words rather than having to quote the exact Bible words.

It's what songwriters do for us. They put the Life-giving Truths of God's word to music for us so that we can sing and meditate on them! They are powerful truths because they are HIS truths. They are His chosen method of changing us from the inside out. The more focused concentration we give to a specific truth, the more impact it will have on us.

It's what preachers and teachers do when they title their sermons and teach the theology drawn from the biblical text.

We are discovering that after a week of working on one truth, it becomes a part of us. We can move on to another truth the next week and still have last week's truth at work in our hearts! It is especially exciting when you go through a whole chapter or book of the Bible pulling out the Life-giving Truth in each section. As you do, its purpose and meaning will come alive to you in ways it never has before. We've all read, studied, and memorized. And now we add the dimension that really brings change!

Now, try it on your own with Romans 12:9-13. Notice that if

you were to try to live out all these instructions out of a heart that didn't possess profound belief in the power of God in you, you would exhaust yourself, be robbed, sapped, and probably become one of those really annoying "do-gooders." Try to identify some truths that will be transforming to the heart. Write them here:

_____

_____

_____

_____

> [1]In case you are curious about your crafting of truth statements, and would find it beneficial to compare yours to what we might do, look to the end of this appendix for our footnoted truth statements.

3. Mark 5:25 – 34   (Drawing truths from the narrative writings of the Bible)
> *This is the account of the bleeding woman who was healed by touching Jesus' clothes in the middle of a crowd.*

A great question to ask of any passage is this:
"What do these words tell me about Jesus?"
"What does He want me to believe about who He is?"

We'll notice that Jesus saw into the woman's heart and was aware of her faith. Many, with great needs, touched Him, yet power went out of Him when she touched Him by faith. We notice the invitation He gave to her, *"Reveal yourself to Me,"* He said.

He could have let her slip into the crowd without even asking who touched Him. He asked, even though He knew, just to give her the opportunity. She was not required to reveal herself! Though she was full of fear and trembling, she identified herself to Him and told Him her whole story. Though He was surrounded by people who wanted His attention and He was on the way to heal someone else, He stopped, looked at her, into her, and intently listened to her story.

As awesome as it is to simply *see* these things about Jesus, there is more. God is inviting us to believe some things on purpose. Things like these:
> "Who I am matters to Jesus."
> "Jesus always has time for me."
> "Jesus wants to hear my whole story."
> "Jesus wants to be face to face."
> "Jesus wants relationship with me today."
> "Jesus can see into my heart."

"Faith unleashes God's power into my life."
"Jesus is inviting me to open myself to Him."
"Jesus doesn't just want to bless me from a distance."

These truths have so much power to bring to my everyday life! But I must take one of them with me into my day/week to work into my heart and train into my values. It won't happen if I hear a sermon on this story. It won't happen if I complete a Bible study on it.

I do so by celebrating it and meditating on it.

I bring about heart-level belief by phrasing a truth statement based in this story and telling myself that truth so constantly throughout each day that finally I actually believe it.

Now it is changing me from the inside out. It will increase my awareness of how wonderful my Savior is and that is a good thing. But life change occurs when His truth becomes my bottom line, heart-level belief system!

4. Genesis 45: 4-15 (Drawing truths from historical writings of the Bible)

This paragraph of scripture is full of powerful Life-giving Truth. As Joseph recounts the story of what his brothers did to him, and how God used it, we are given something life-changing to believe. Joseph's brothers sold him into slavery out of selfishness and hatred. It was a very evil thing that happened and yet Joseph can see that God was behind it!

He says in verse 8, *"It was not you who sent me here, but God."* His words are written to reveal to us that God is in control of everything and is both willing and able to use evil to accomplish His good purposes (Romans 8:28; Genesis 50:20).

Here are some ways to simply state the truths of this passage:
God is willing and able to use evil.
People don't determine the circumstances of my life.
God determines the circumstances of my life.
God is writing the story.
There is something bigger going on right now.
God is always doing something.
God is the one in control.
I can let go of the hurt people cause me.
I can trust God in everything!
I don't have to take revenge.
I can forgive.
I must be willing to hurt so God can work out His plan.
I have to let God be God.
People don't have ultimate power over me.

Wow! Those are truths with power! Truth we desperately

need! Many who are reading this appendix, I'm willing to bet, were raised on these incredible Bible stories. Do you see the additional power using a story's truths could have for life transformation?

What might happen if we chose to believe any one of these truths in all the little moments of life that are difficult, frustrating, disappointing and even painful? Somehow it's easier to go there with huge crisis, but every "typical" difficulty gives us a chance to practice believing what is true instead of what our feelings or the world tells us!

In fact, why don't you consider the story of Samson (Judges 16), or of Daniel in the lion's den (in the book by his name), or Elijah (1 Kings 18) and the prophets of Baal and write your Life-giving Truths here:

_____

_____

_____

[2] Compare yours...

5. Isaiah 58 (Drawing truths from the prophetical writings of the Bible)

The subject is fasting. Ask as you read, "What does God want me to believe about fasting?" The next step is where it gets exciting and personal. Ask what God wants me to believe about myself, about life, about Him, about spiritual life, about people, from this teaching around fasting.

You could spend your time researching the history of fasting in the Older Testament, the Newer Testament, and in Church History or world religions. There would be some benefit to the storing of that knowledge I'm sure. Or you could fast. You could plan and do. But if your belief system doesn't change then the information is soon set aside and the behavior fizzles out eventually. Fond memories of a season of fasting investigation and experimentation, and nothing more.

But if you allow truth to believe to give your knowledge wings and your actions depth of meaning, then you will experience authentic heart change.

Here is a list of some truths to believe from this passage:
vv. 2, 3 "God won't honor spiritual-looking, selfish behavior."
"Words alone are empty."
"Spiritual activities by themselves are meaningless."
"God sees through me to my deepest motives."
v. 6 "I really need God to change my heart."
"If God doesn't change my heart, I can't honor Him."
vv. 6-9 "God is looking for surrender, and repentance."

vv. 6-10 *"Real spiritual life changes who I am."*
v. 9 *"I need to be honest with myself."*
v. 11 *"Real life comes with repentance and surrender."*
v. 13 *"I always have to check my heart."*

6. Matthew 5: 3-12 (Drawing truths from Jesus' teachings in the Bible)

Looking closely at what has become known as The Beatitudes, let's ask what God is inviting us to believe. This gets us to the heart of why Jesus spoke. These words call us to think in stark contrast to how we naturally think and the way the world has taught us to think.

Consider these Life-giving Truths:
It's good if I don't get what I want.
It's good for me to hurt.
Being sinned against is a great opportunity.
When life leaves me empty, I'm in the best place.
Being persecuted for my faith is a privilege!
The chance to swallow my pride is a gift.
God wants to keep me hungry for more.

Does this give you eyes to see the difference between what God calls us to believe, as we live our daily lives, and what we actually believe? Can you taste the transforming and life-giving power of these truths?

7. Revelation 5:1-5 (Drawing truths from the Apocalyptic writings of the Bible)

Consider these Life-giving Truths:
I can't fully understand how much I need Jesus.
Jesus is the ONLY one able to give eternal life.
Everyone has a desperate need for Jesus.
My end is determined by Jesus.
Our eternal destiny is dependent on Jesus.
I need Jesus.
Only Jesus is enough.
I can't face death without Jesus.
My hope is in Jesus now and forever.
Jesus is the only real hope we have.
Everyone needs Jesus.
No one will make it to heaven without Jesus.

Here is a great example of how we can glean life-altering truth from difficult-to-understand passages. The context of these words will reveal who the Lion is, that He is also the Lamb that was slain, and that He is Jesus, our final Judge.

But here's the deal: we can still read this passage, all by itself, and find truth to believe that will change our lives. It is not a scholarly approach, and though some cling to a certain form of Christian arrogance about that knowledge, even claiming that we can't grow without what they call "deeper study," or "digging in," or "drilling down," or "moving on from the milk to eat meat," the reality is that God wanted every person who is His throughout history to glean truth no matter what section of Scripture they might have access to at any given moment. He made it accessible to the uneducated and simple. People like me!

It goes back to Paul's words about knowledge making us arrogant, and about the foolish discussions we promote on finer points of theology in the name of maturity and orthodoxy.

All we're suggesting is that God intended for us to see Him and believe something transformational whenever we open the Bible and it is easier than we think.

So, none of us has taken to heart or yet understood the place that God has given to Jesus and our desperate need for Him. We never will, fully, until the time comes...until He comes again. Yet the opportunity lies before us to drive home to our own hearts His powerful position and our deep need. These are the seeds from which true love grows.

Day by day as we contemplate truths like those we gleaned above, our hearts will fall more and more in love with Jesus, and that is the point. It is the bottom line. Not knowledge, but love. And we will learn to live in awe and wonder. We will be conquered by the Word, rather than settling for merely conquering the word.

It is so easy for us to humanize Jesus, the LORD OF ALL, and see Him as a really nice person who did something really nice for us. So now, logically, we owe Him. How short that falls! How important to permanently alter our unconscious beliefs so as to actually see Him more clearly, more fully, finally being consumed by Him, as are all the heavenly beings we read about throughout the book of Revelation!

That is the goal of Life-giving Truth.

Conclusion:

Once you have learned to find Life-giving Truth, you can continue to work the 4 Life-giving Practices into whatever groups, Bible Studies, or classes that you are involved in. The only adjustment you'll have to make is to reserve time for all four practices. You'll also have to leave time in the context of your discussion/study to determine the Life-giving Truth you will take with you as you leave! It is very unifying when a group works on the same truth, and even more so when a whole church does! It can also be challenging to listen each week to the ways people processed a truth different from yours.

One of the greatest benefits comes when you invite family members, roommates, or accountability partners to work your truth with you! That way you can help remind each other and play a part in another person's growth! You can search out a Life-giving Truth from every message you hear and actually work at taking that message to heart and watch God change you through it. I used to see the Bible as a "sword" that we can use to change ourselves. You know, slicing, dicing, even doing major surgery of the heart. My effort and skill at applying God's word to my life.

But as I looked more closely I noticed that it is called the "sword of the Spirit" (Ephesians 6). It is the weapon God uses to conquer our hearts (Hebrews 4:12, 13). Our goal as we approach God's word is not to conquer it, by figuring out what it says and means or even how it all fits together. Our goal is to invite God's Holy Spirit to do His conquering work in us by using the eternal and transforming truths of His word.

Footnotes...

[1] Truth statements from Romans 12:9-13...
Behavior is only good if it comes from a loving heart; There is no fence between evil and good; Love gives its life away; It's never time to give up; Love leaves no room for selfishness; Life is best when devoted to others; Life can't be about me; I serve the Lord when I love people; When I honor people, God is honored.

[2] Truth statements from...
...the story of Samson:
Strength comes from God alone; God uses broken people; God can bring good results out of bad choices; God works miracles in real people.
...the story of Daniel:
I can stand alone; God will use me for great things; God will give us spiritual insight; I can tell the truth no matter the consequences; God will be exalted above all; Man has no power God didn't give him; Bad things happen to good people; God uses all things for good.
...the story of Elijah:
Doing God's work is exhausting;
Judgment is sure;
>   (Theological truths are good, but they can keep our thinking on a theoretical level. We feel that personal truths are more transforming for day-to-day living)

No risk is too great;
I can be part of a miracle;
My face belongs between my knees;
I can open my eyes to the coming work of God.

Other books by Neal & Judy Brower...

<u>Simple Devotion</u> – facing seven foundations for inviting women to intimacy with Jesus
<u>Simple Devotion Workbook</u> – a workbook for personal and small group application.
<u>Pray&Watch</u> – focusing on Life-giving Impact

Future projects...
<u>Walking Worship</u> – focusing on Life-giving Prayer
<u>Inside Out</u> – focusing on Life-giving Truth
<u>Unbroken Heart</u> – focusing on Life-giving Relationships
<u>The Life-giving Lifestyle</u> – bringing it all together

Neal and/or Judy are also available for your conference, retreat, seminar and training events. Feel free to contact them to discuss details and arrangements.

Visit us at:
www.simplelivinginc.net